" Life is a adventure" with God at the wheel

Our journey on the paths God
has before us are unknown by us,

But fully planned out for us by a very loving God,
This is story of life on and at times off the path God had
for my life, becoming His masterpiece.

Written By Minister, Susan K. Moll

DEDICATION PAGE

When I was thinking who to dedicate this book to, I looked at my others, it was friends, family and husband, but this one is a little different, I thank my mom and dad for having me and raising me the way they did,

I may have not liked it at the time but am so very thankful for the lessons they taught me, and to my Heavenly Father who with gentle hands lead me, protected me, corrected me and molded me into who I am now.

And my dear children, they had to go through so very much for all my lessons to be taught. They had to suffer from time to time as they watched me go through things so I could grow. I love you all so very much and am so proud of the adults you have grown in to.

My precious husband Tom, he has shown me what it is to have love in your marriage, to be lifted up and not cut down, to be cared for and not hurt, to have them to allow you to let your feelings out with out getting mad at you for having a view, I love you so much .

I thank my pastor and his wife Deana so very much, he has allowed to Lord to speak through him to my heart, with words I know were meant for my heart to hear and heal. And Deana for her knowledge in editing. This is to every person that has touched my life.

Whether in person, on face book, or just passing on the street, you have touch my heart and life in some way or the other and this is for you, for ex husbands, and ex in-laws, friends near and ones far away.

This is dedicated to you for you all have made me who I am today.

There will be some places for you to fill in the blanks, please do this so you can

remember and also when you grow you can see how your answers change with you.

TITLES IN ORDER

MY JOURNEY

A LITTLE ABOUT THE MINISTRY

MY TESTIMONY

LET THE WORSHIPERS ARISE

GOD OR MEDICINE

FAITH AND UNSEEN ILLNESSES

HOLINESS OF GOD

HOW GREAT IS OUR GOD

DO YOU KNOW A LOST LAMB

WHY PRAYER WORKS

BACK TO THE BASICS

FISHERS OF MAN

THE DREADED RECLINER

HOW TO AVOID THE PITY PARTY

IN MOUNTAIN AND VALLEY I WILL PROTECT YOU

DONT LET THE DEVIL WIN WITH DEPRESSION

WHEN CHRISTIANS HAVE DOUBT

A CLOAK FOR YOUR SINS

CALLED FOR A PURPOSE

WHAT DO OTHERS SEE

DONT BE DECEIVED

REAL LIFE IS OUR DAYS AREN'T PROMISED

GOD'S HEALTHCARE PLAN

KNOWING OUR LIMITS

REMOVING YOUR VEIL

FALLING OF ANGELS

BEING TRANSFORMED,

MY JOURNEY

When I started to put this book together in June of 2012, I had to stop and think how I got to this point in my life,all the stuff I had to live through,cry through and pray through, I am 56 years old this year.

I had gone through 4 marriages,three children, gone through being involved in white magic,card reading,stone worship through crystals,being abused,homeless,and yet.

God never gave up on me, for all the years I searched,for the right man to fill this empty void I had in my life, I would see qualities in a man and think, wow man of my dreams, be swayed by their charm into their bed and into marriage.

Then the change in them came out and I saw the man they pretended to be wasn't who they really were inside, again I would go out searching for the perfect man,only to find after years of searching, human man wasn't what was missing in my life..it was Jesus.

It's as if its my life was a puzzle and Jesus is the missing piece, you can try as hard as you want to try and make other pieces fit in the empty spot, but only one will fill the void spot perfectly.

From the time I was in high school, God was working full time to keep a eye on me and keep me safe. I had been doing things that could have killed me, falling off bluffs at Hawn state park, but drunk enough and high enough I didn't get hurt.

Being in situations that got me raped but not killed, again drunk, drove home alone in car of man that had raped me cause he passed out, never been behind the wheel of a car before,parked it down street and walked, but knew I had to get back home and back in my window before my parents knew I wasn't in my room.

Could never say anything to them for support on what had happened because they had told me never to leave and go out of town with him.

I had snuck out of my room by climbing down TV antenna pole by my window, and drunk made it home and in my room without them ever knowing. (at only 16)

I quit drinking the whole time I was married to my first husband,at 21 but after we got divorced I felt so alone and unloved, I had two children and now was in charge of them alone.

I worked, came home,cooked and cleaned, read stories to them, sewed their clothes and for Christmas made their toys I was trying so hard to be a good mommy.

I then met my second husband, we lived across the street from each other, I would play baseball with my kids and all the neighbor kids after school.

One day Zach asked him to come over to play ball, he played ball and stayed for super, he liked the cooking I guess cause he came back everyday till I married him.
(at 30)

After the first year I had a son and we were raising 3 kids, we bought a house and had a dog and cat, flowers in the flowerbeds..the perfect setting.

But when the love of his life got her divorce and was a free lady, he wasn't wanting to be married any longer, so once again I was divorced.(at 35)

So by the age of 35 I had been married twice,divorced twice and had three children,this is when the drinking started back up.

I got sitters,went out dancing and to parties with friends, and now I needed a glass of wine to unwind after work,to sleep,to deal with stress,to watch TV.

My family never knew because I was taught how to hide it from them, but I wasn't hiding it from my kids, they saw and watched there mother become something they were ashamed of.

I also started smoking,you know its funny, when your the one doing all this, you can make reasons why its ok, why its not hurting anyone. but its all a big lie.

How many times did I drive my children home drunk, a 5 mile ride not even knowing how I got home, what all they saw and what all they heard I will never really know, because sometimes I couldn't remember.

I would put them to bed and watch TV with a wine cooler in hand, one night I thought all 3 were asleep, I went to get a drink and I was out, I looked all over and there wasn't any in the house.

I went in and looked at the kids, all 3 sound asleep, I would just jump in the car go down to the corner and get a 6 pack and be home in a few seconds, they would never even know I was gone.

I didn't think about other people checking out, talking and joking around while I was waiting in line, my 30 second trip was more like 20 min.

I walked into the house and there in the middle of the floor in tears was my baby Timmy, he ran to me, mommy I so scared, I couldn't find you,I picked him up and was never so ashamed of myself..my life..what could have happened.

I held him and put him back to bed in my room, poured every bottle out and held him all night, this time I was in tears.

Its so painful to even remember this to write it down but I know I have to for you to know where I was, my third marriage was a very short one, I started dating because it was a friend of a friend, he was sweet but so set in his ways, a family just wasn't in his life and within 3 years it was over.(at 40)

Where I was now working there was a man working there and as we talked and shared things with me, it seemed so unreal, he knew what I was going through, was so interested in what I was doing with the bible studies I was having, understood all the situations in my life and in all this I never knew till much later, he was studying me, asking people that knew me, what does she like, what are her interests,learning all about me so he could be the perfect person for me. And I believed him.

I never understood how he could control me so much and talk me into just about anything, back to drinking, pot, doing card readings, never ever to say no to him,if I did I would see brown eyes turn black in anger. he was a con artist and I had been one of his subjects. After I was away from him people told me what he had done, he had studied me for months before he ever made his move.

The next 10 years would be a living hell on earth, the man I was married to was a drug abuser,dealer,and very much into black magic to control people.

I can say this because its in public records and they are still being made on him. I pray for him now that his eyes will be opened and somehow come to see his path of death if changes aren't made soon.

I may have not been able to reach him but pray someone will and save him from himself, that's something Jesus can do, he can take someone that hurt you in so many ways and allow the pain to turn to compassion.

I was abused, in so very ways, used, forced to do things that shamed me beyond words just not to make him mad, and homeless for 7 months all because of his drug habits. after 10 years and many times of being so near death from blood sugar problems to thoughts of just ending it all.

God was always with me, any time I cried out to Him..please just show me your here, I am so scared so alone I just need to see your here. He would show up in ways it could only be a God thing.

Once when it just to be more than I thought I could handle anymore, I walked out in the lake, anyone that knows me knows my fear of water over my head, but this time was different,the water was sort of calling to me.

Come out to the deep,walk out, no more pain,no more hurting, no more fear, only peace, just let go walk out deeper, up to my chin,so close to giving up and going on out.

At that very second this little fish jumps out of water right in front of me,flips its tail slaps me on the cheek and goes down in the water, God said as clear as a bell. That man has taken everything away, don't you dare let him take your life. I came out of water determined to find way out.

When asking for God to show me if the time was right for me to move on and go back to Missouri, I knew if it wasn't in His timing things wouldn't fall in place, but if it was His time it would work out perfect.

He sent thousands of Monarch butterflies landing on me, covering the sky to the point it caused a shadow over where I was sitting,when I asked what is this!! my then husband told me, its time for the butterflies to migrate, God was telling me it was my time also.

When so afraid I went to hide in chicken coop, sometimes I would cry and pray, wanting so much just to feel His presence, to know I wasn't alone. With all 3 of my children gone for the week end, my husband was on one of his many drug runs.

Not knowing what he would be like when he got home I went to the coop, God I need to know your here, I need a hug to let me know it will be ok, I am so scared God, so very scared.

At that very moment my big dog Zen came to me and put his paws around me and held on so tight, I hugged him back so tight knowing it was another God moment.

As the years past and I went to Arkansas. To find my roots and see if there was a way to go back to your home town and find where you could call home.

What I found was away from my family and friends I became a prisoner in my own home and after a year we lost that home do to all our money going for bad things and not rent.

Homeless at lake Ouachita near Denby point, I was there for 7 months, during that time I learned so much about myself, I could get a fire going even after a heavy rain for my morning coffee. :)

I made sections for a house, I had a living room with remnants of carpet a friend gave me, kitchen area, changing tent and sleeping tent,bathroom area with sheets for walls, had 2, 5 gal bag lined buckets to potty in, where at end of day I would dig a 18 inch deep hole to bury it.

I had mirror on tree with bakers rack to hold my make up and bowl to wash face and brush my teeth, I may be homeless but to anyone going by or in town when I got to go, I would never look like it, I would always look clean.

I washed clothes in the lake and dried them on trees, fished daily and learned to filet a fish and found out I could have made a pretty good girl scout.

But when left alone for days with no food,clean water and only cooler of hot beer that made me sick ,in 108 weather,no shade well it wasn't good, with low blood sugar in a very short time I was in trouble.

Two very dear friends Randy and Becky would always come check on me at least every other day, so glad she did that day, I was very close to heat exhaustion and blood sugar bottoming out.

When my husband finally showed back up they wouldn't let me go with him, he was told you get her back home to Mo. or we will.

I found a way home through friends in Arkansas. I was able to get a job, get certified as CMA and restorative therapy assistant, got a great job and made enough that I was able to get a divorce from him, get my own place and get back on the right track..Gods path

Within 6 months after my divorce I ran into a friend I had a crush on in 10th grade but never got to date him, we ran into each other at McDonald's we talked a little and went our own ways.

After a few weeks we made calls to each other and he asked if he could date me, I told him I wasn't really ready to date but he could come over for a meal and we could go through old pictures to catch up on our lives since high school.

We had great evening and after awhile we dated, but not for long,but the really awesome thing that came from that short time together was he took me to the church his nephew preached at the Remnant church in Ste Genevieve.

When we got there I was so awe struck, it was the old Baptist church I grew up in, was baptized in, married the first time in, as I walked in the doors I knew.

It may look different on the inside, the pews are gone, and cushioned chairs are there, the place I was baptized is gone and its now a praise and worship area, there now carpet with a beautiful cross inlaid in the aisle.

But the same God lives there, the over whelming feeling of welcome home my child just poured all over me, they start to sing,"I'm coming back to the heart of worship"

As tears rolled down my cheeks I knew no matter what, I was never leaving the church and my time with other believers, the sermons were like God talking to my heart, I would never walk away from this again.

I had prayer with this one man there and he was so sweet and shy, but over time when we greeted each other our hands seemed like it took longer to let go.

One day he asked if he could come over and work on my jeep and see if he could get it running for me, also he was working with my youngest son on his guitar.

I had to get emergency surgery a few weeks after we decided to try to date, he took off a week of work to take care of me, he would leave when my sister or son were going to be there because I wasn't suppose to be alone for awhile, he cooked, cleaned, and took the best care of me and I think this was the time we knew we were going to be together for a long time.(at 51)

We were married and have been in our own little heaven on earth, we both know we were created for each other, but we got off to a rough start.

In April of 2008 my momma passed away, then just a few months later his momma passed away, we would now be strength to each other with this time of grief.

Our first anniversary was spent in ER from him being in accident when his van was hit from behind. he was able to go home that evening but made a memory not soon to be forgotten.

We have become grandma and grandpa to my daughter's son in 2009 and are learning as the years go by that life really is like a box of chocolates, you never know what you are going to get.

I have learned that we always have to wait on God's timing for things to fall into place, once I felt lead to start a homeless shelter, just knew I was being lead, I gathered clothes and supplies, made fliers to put out, had meal plans and researched where the area was that didn't have any shelters. I had it planned I knew it was right, but every door I tried would close in my face.

Why it was a me thing and not a God thing, we have to pray and allow time for God to talk to us, when we try to say ok God I have it from here..it wont work, when its His will doors open and things will fall into place.

I can't say that all my life was bad, I have many childhood memories that are so special to me,times I know people would have wished they could have kept me behind locked doors hehe.

When a 5 year old is let out to play and the boss of my dad lived a few houses down, and they left their dachshund outside with a gal of green paint and a brush, in my head she would be beautiful the same color as their garage they had just painted.

The awful knock at the door and the voice saying very strong, was Susan outside today, there were people that had sugar put in gas tanks just to see if the whole bag would fit in that little hole.

But you know what when dad went to retirement parties for fellow workers, guess who they asked about, whats that little Susie up to these days, boy she was a handful wasn't she, they never forgot me and dad never got fired over it.

You see we lived in company houses with a huge field between where the pump house was and the houses, when the whistle blew that work was over, out I went to meet my daddy and the boss.

None of the other kids did that, they were scared of him cause their dad's worked for him, not me I don't think at that time in my life I wasn't scared of anything, that's probably what got me in the most trouble.

When a boy came down the street with a wagon full of puppies and after we played for awhile I got in his wagon, he told me to get out, I wanted to stay with the puppies,he picked up a piece of wood and hit me on the side of my head.

The nail missed my eye by just a few centimeters, after getting a few stitches I also got the boys wagon and he got grounded, I had 7 black eyes before I was ever in school and one for jr pictures.

I was always one you could never tell me I wasn't able to do something because that just made me want to try, when my third husband told me I couldn't take his worm box out of the garden area, I decided if it stayed it was going to be pretty.

    I taught myself to paint with q-tips and cotton balls and the started using his sheet rock from some of his remodeling in garage he was doing. I got a few brushes and taught myself to paint anything I saw.

    With time I would paint to music and in a years time I had 97 paintings all over my walls, a gallery in our second living-room, with animals, landscapes,Indian pictures and a few of family members.

    I painted so many things to music and it was also good therapy, the best storm over a ocean was right after divorce and all the feelings of hurt and betrayal came out in the storm and was let go.

    I have won 1st place with many of them at fairs and best of show for my sun set at the lake, some I have sold and some I still have, many hang on my walls today as reminders of things I saw or went through.

    A few years ago I had to give up the smaller detail painting due to getting arthritis in my wrist along with carpal tunnel. But the visions were so amazing, some of my work when I took them to fairs to show, people would come up to me and tell me they knew where that was.

    Things I saw in my head they had been there, in doing in-home care for a couple in Arkansas, the man told me the painting of dream home was his sister in Ohio's land and home, even the pond in the front, when they passed away the daughter came to return the painting I ended up letting him have,I told her to give it to his sister, they were so happy.

    I never went any farther that high school, in 1975 I went to the Pima Medical institute for about 6 months, but do to lack time for then husband I had to quit ,we got to the part of working 40 hours in hospital for training and I wouldn't have been able to work as CMA and go to school too.

    I did work in nursing homes for over 15 years, worked in factories and drove school bus for 5 years, I loved meeting people and talking to them, I now work as tour guide at historic home in my home town in summer months and museum winter months.

    Even when I was homeless, there were some things that I really want to remember and cherish, like early morning times, I would get up before it was very light out, gather kindling for the fire, then another trip to get bigger sticks and get the fire going.

Then I went to the edge of the lake, sat on a big log that was there and have prayer, sometimes with tears, sometimes just amazed at the beauty of the sun coming up over the tree.

There would be a light mist and the sun would hit the droplets of water, and sparkle down to the water, it looked like tiny diamonds floating and landing on the water and then the birds would start singing, fish jumping out of the water to get bugs.

I had my dads telescope and it made it like the discovery channel, you could watch eagles and hawks swoop down and get a fish and take it to a tree limb and eat, like it was about 10 ft away.

Once I saw something in the lake that looked like a shark, I knew there wasn't any so I went and got the scope, it was a deer, I never knew a deer could swim across a lake to a small island and to see it shake off just like a dog was so awesome.

I would also lay the fish net out at the edge of water and put fish food on it, scoop up tiny fish to go fishing with later on in the day, I had a minnow bucket in the water and would use them about 10 am when I got fish for the day.

Well every once in awhile the bucket would be empty if I sat it out over night. So I decided to watch and see what was getting in my bucket, about 4 am a heron came in and would go into the top with its long beak and eat the fish.

I also found out if you leave a box of worms in the shade you will get attacked by blue jays when you go try to get them out, had to start covering it to keep them out, so much to look back on and smile.

I didn't know how to swim so I had the idea in shallow water I could teach myself, I put a tire I found down and walked off 15 feet and laid another one and would dog paddle from one to the other till I got tired.

Well, one day I had gone back a forth about 10 times, 5 more and I was done, I saw something out of the side of my eye beside me and lowered my legs to stand, it was a HUGE fish, a carp about the size of a small bass boat. (not a pretty fish)

It just stayed there, so slowly I swam back again, it stayed by my side and did for the last 5 laps, I was scared but thought if it was going to hurt me it would have by now, when the last lap was done I stood up and it slowly swam away, the closest I will ever get to swimming with a dolphin.

Fish got huge do to the fact at the dam on the other side was a fishery, the left over food when the systems were flushed ended up at the base of the dam, that was a feeding spot for catfish and carp all ground feeders. 82 lbs catfish were caught there.

It was so fun watching my dogs play, my little Tinkerbell was so scared but would come to me in the water, she would hold on to me like a baby and I would walk around with her so she cold get a bath.

Chinook my 65 lb white lab knew her fear and when they would go to the waters edge for a drink, he would walk over to her and dunk her head under, she would run to me and I would have to dry her face.

He had no fear of anything, he jumped in the water from little bluffs on the edge and you could show him a rock, throw it in the water and he would find it, I would mark it with a marker to be able to tell.

My cat Milo would be my little warrior, he would go get things and being so very proud of his kill leave it at the edge of my tent, I would find squirrels, rats, and one time a possum , he got a very bad bite from that one and in the end that's what killed him, it got very infected, after I got back to Mo I took him to vet, it had gang green in it and after surgery to remove it just never recovered...awesome cat.

My life has always been a adventure, never knowing what was going to happen as my son told me one time, we had him for the winter break and on the way home hit some black ice in Little Rock, the jeep spun out and after about 6 spins ended up on the other side of medium facing oncoming traffic, the jeep stopped at the edge of the road.

Because of the bad weather we decide to just stay at hotel, well so did everyone else, no opening any place, we drove around and ended up lost on ice covered road in the back of really bad area.

We saw a church and I said I know someone will help us there..no space, but there was a man walking and we asked if he knew a place we could stay for a few hours till day light. He said stay put and he would ask his sister up the street.

When he came back he said we could stay there for 25 bucks, we agreed, got there talked to her and she told us where we could stay, the room was cold, dirty and only had a bucket for toilet.

After a hour we were woke up with a knock on door, she was going to need more money, after going out to see what they were talking about found cooking crack and they needed drug money and it was going to cost us 30 more dollars.

We said we didn't have it and left again. Weren't going to pay for there habit, we spent night at gas station parking lot, we had 30 more mile to home. At day light we set out, we got to the outer side of Hot springs and trees were down over all the roads for the next 8 miles.

Trucks were out cutting them down to make way for ambulance on other side, as the ambulance came through three more trees fell, and they closed the road, we now had to go back 10 miles to Glenwood turn off .

After weaving in and out of trees, moving them off the road we made it to Mt Ida and our road, but you couldn't drive it, trees down, no electric nothing, we walked a mile with our stuff and made it home, our animals were all ok

But we had nothing, we built a fire in fire pit, put blanket up in hallway to keep any heat we could get in the one area, a tree had come through roof so we had ventilation for our space heater, we had propane heat in a trailer for heat and our cook-stove.

With only one room heat we stayed in the one room, reading stories to each other, played board games, Yahtzee, card games like war and go fish so much fun for a 10 year old and his mommy. playing with the animals all under the covers, took walks in daylight to see the ice covering everything, it was so beautiful, made the woods around us look like a ice palace sparkling like diamonds on all the trees, roads and for 2 weeks it was like this, after that they were able to make it back with the electric trucks and get it turned back on.

But when we had the lights come back Tim looked so sad, I said Timmy honey what is it, he looked up at me and said its over now, the cuddling, reading stories, getting to keep Tinky in bed with us, our adventure is over, I reached up and turned the lights off, got flashlight and said no it isn't.

Those times taught me what was really important, it was the amount of time you have with each other, it's the quality of time, that time when your child feels like they are so loved, so protected any way you can and make everyday a adventure for them.

These times made a treasured memory for both of us that we will never forget and even though he is 23 now, those memories are price less for both of us. Times he knew he was number one, and he didn't have to fight anyone for my attention. Even now it makes me smile.

My husband Tom and I are going to be married 5 years in a few months and its been the best of my life. In those 5 years,we have worked, been laid off in 2010 and only working part time, have gone from a house to senior apartments and have had 2 of my books published.

My first book was published in 2010 "**New Beginnings Ministry**" and the second one the following May, " **Your Transformation Into A Butterfly**" they are more devotionals, bible studies that I had taught from 1996 on.

Then in 2012 **"Finding your Healing"** came into play, dealing with chronic pain everyday and what goes through your head, your heart and your spirit and the outcome if you don't see it for what it is, it distorts the way you think feel and live your life and how it effects those loves ones around you.

Then the **revised addition of "New Beginning's Ministry"** in 2010 when I wrote my first book, I had no idea yet of what to do, how to present it, and it was so full of mistakes, wrong wording and so to get the book in the right presentation form and with better devotionals I redid this book. Also in 2012

I love to write and so when I received this calling God took a gift He had blessed me with, the gift of placing thoughts to paper, turning pain to blessing and anger to compassion, allowing Him to use me to share with the world, how very much He loves you and wants to bless you if you only trust and love Him.

In this book I wanted to share a few more devotionals but also take time to share how I got to this point in my life, that God can use anyone no matter how bad you have been to share His word and try to lead others to know Him and how much He loves you.

I was such a sinner and had been the sort of person not to many people could understand or get close to, But God saw the heart and knew He could mold me into a useable vessel.

I have been on His potters wheel many times and so many times He had to smash the clay and start over, but each time He would start over there would be a little less He had to fix, the more willing I became the more He could use me.

At this point in my life I am so open to do His will, each day I am given I ask when I wake up, what do ya want to do today Jesus, I am ready. when we are open to His leadership we become a instrument He can use .

It's a day by day thing, you do the very best you can each and every day, yes you will make mistakes we aren't perfect and we will slip up, but as soon as you know you have, just ask forgiveness and mean it, don't keep messing up just cause you know you will be forgiven, but mean it and don't make that same sin again.

I always heard that God knew us and had plans for our lives from the very moment of conception, with what I found the other day I believe that even more than I did, when I was being born, the lady that was in the labor room with mom gave her a gift, it was two little pins made of gold.

Mom gave them to me a very long time ago because of the way they came to her, but with the things I have shared and how God has spoken to me so many times with them, does it really surprise you they were two little butterflies?

The free time God has blessed us with will be to give Him all the glory, I praise Him with hands held high and say here I am, your vessel ready to be filled up with your spirit to pour out to a dry and thirsty land.

Big Hugs to the world
Susie Sunshine

A LITTLE ABOUT MY MINISTRY AND ME

My name is Susan Moll, (Susie sunshine) to all my friends, I became a ordained minister in 1996. I have created websites and wrote books for this reason. when I was first saved and wanting to change my life around, I needed to find out how to change the things in my life I no longer wanted to be a part of.

The only real way to change was to read the word and try to find a way to apply it to my life today, in doing this I have grown and have learned to be open to Gods leadership in my life.

In about 2006 my son set me up with a myspace account, in that he told me I could make my page anyway I want to, I knew I wanted to have it a testimony page, in a weeks time I had over 800 people comment on bible studies I was posting, people all over the world.

I knew then I was really doing what I was called to do in 1996, to reach the world and share how much God loves them,I made 6 other sites since then with studies, devotions, and just share what God is doing in my life.

Then in 2010 I published my first book " New Beginnings Ministry " and later that same year " Your Transformation Into A Butterfly " I have been so blessed from the response I have received from people that have read them.

So this ministry is to help new Christians or others that are just searching to see how we can relate what we read in the bible to our lives today, If I can help just one person that is searching for a answer, then God has used my hands , heart and mind to get His words out.

This isn't about me, its about allowing God to flow through you, He places things in my heart and I pray about it, He then shows me the scriptures and guides me to put it together so I can get it out to you.

My prayer is to always be a vessel He can fill up to over flowing so I can pour it out to my readers. you can write to me at

(dragonfly5918@sbcglobal.net)or you can post questions to me on here.
      I will answer each one personally and as quickly as I can, If I don;t know the answer, I will search the word till I find it, everything is based on the word, not mine.
I hope this has given you a little idea of why I am here, its for you.
love in Christ to all of you ..Susie

 the chains I had on me from my sinful life were broken and I was free from the way they held me down, with the Holy Spirit now in my life and in control I had a purpose in my life that was driven with a desire to share with anyone that I could, of His love, this forgiveness that was beyond all my understanding.

the Peace of knowing He is waiting with open arms the day I am called home to be with Him.. the latest victory He has given me is with my smoking, here is that testimony.

MY TESTIMONY, THE SMOKING DEMON

Today is the 21st of June 2012 and also the 39th month of being a non smoker, I have smoked for most of my life, quit for 15 years, went back after divorce in 85, quit for 6 months here, 3 months there but couldn't let the stupid things go.

I wanted to quit so much, I prayed, had others pray and lay hands on me only to go home and lite up another, this happened so many times, each time I felt like I had let myself down, let others down and most of all let God down.

So why is this time different, because I can now fight what I never had seen before. Over the last few days and the past 2 weeks before, my heart was really feeling the conviction of the smoking, I would think of the things I have yet to do in my life and the things I want accomplish.

With my book going out and having my name on the cover,"MINISTER" Susan K Moll, what sort of witness is that for Jesus to go around with a cigarette in my mouth, a sinning minister, I know there were sins in my life but this is one I could do something about, I want to be a vessel for God to use a clean vessel.

I would lite a cigarette up and see it as one day less I would have, I said ok God show me how to let this go. Well what I had to see was this, I had people explain, it is a addictive spirit, a oppressive spirit, well what I saw is this, if its a addictive or oppressive spirit, it isn't of God, if the spirit isn't of God its from the devil which would make it a demon.

So now it had a name to be called out of me, it is a demonic spirit of smoking, knowing this I went to my pastor, I told him what I felt and that on Easter Sunday I wanted to give this up. And was asking for prayer for me to be ready and really let it go.

Well he asked me if I was sure, and if I was sure, why not just go on and do it that night, our Wednesday evening service, well I knew I wanted it gone, out of me now and I was ready. We were singing blessed be the name and when we got to the verse He gives and takes away, I could see Him giving me the strength to let this addiction go and taking the demon from me.

The ladies came and prayed over me, calling the demon out, healing my lungs, clearing my body of the toxins that had been placed there by the cigarettes, I felt God flow through me so very strong, so strong I couldn't stand up any longer. They gently laid me down and continued to pray over me, I was so very weak but in a good way,

I knew the demon was now out of me, and would never be allowed in this body again. this was March 15th 2010

Well after telling my son Tim what had happened, on Friday he said well lets get you really healthy mom, lets go for a walk, sure lets get Isabelle and go, well we walked and I was going to take pictures of the water coming up, we got to the bridge where I was normally out of breath.

Still breathing fine, went on all the very back of the marina, I think about a mile or so, not real sure, but took pictures and walked back, STILL not out of breath still feeling fine, I know when I was delivered from the smoking I was also healed of the damage I had caused to my body. Yes my calf hurt and my back was hurting, Isabelle's little feet hurt but I was breathing, and felt so good, I have had 3 times that it was really hard, but I have life savers, carrot sticks, and healthy things, and I also have the gum when I just want to be able to hold on and am feeling really weak, I have had to use the gum a few times (3 times), but will NEVER pick up a cigarette again.

I have healthy things to take the place of the habit of having something in my hand I wont start eating things for comfort unless its a vegetable or fruit, I will take care of the vessel God is wanting to use.

I will treat it like its special, I want others to see Jesus in me and I wont make Jesus live in something that smelling of cigarettes, or anything that would not be pleasant to him.

If you have come to the point you really want to give this up, call it by its name and cast it out, call on friends that have gone through this, have them talk you through the hard times, pray for you daily, it can be done, but only if God is in the center of it.

I pray that you wont let pride keep you from telling your friends you need help, cause you know what, they already know, you can try to hide it but they know, you cant cover the smell, and they also know even if your a christian the devil can find a weakness to come into your spirit, please be strong enough to close this one door.

With prayers for everyone that is going through this with me,

we can do this together, your not alone.

LET THE WORSHIPERS ARISE

THE WORSHIPERS ARISE..WHAT A SONG TO START THE NEW YEAR WITH, TO SURRENDER TO THE KING THIS DAY... AS I AWOKE AND WENT INTO FIX MY COFFEE, JOY FM WAS PLAYING .. LET THE WORSHIPERS ARISE, LET YOUR SONS AND YOUR DAUGHTERS SING, I'M SURRENDERING MY ALL..I SURRENDER TO MY KING, LETS ALL SURRENDER OUR LIVES THIS 1ST DAY OF THE NEW YEAR, SURRENDER TO OUR KING..JESUS

Ecclesiastes 8:7 Ecc 8:7 Indeed, they do not know what is to be, for who can tell them how it will be?

Galatians 6:9. Gal 6:9 So let us not grow weary in doing what is right, for we will reap at harvest time, if we do not give up.

    Do it with all your heart, don't give up when things don't go right, keep up with it, keep trying till it works, the rewards will be yours when you do. . "Let us not become weary in doing good, for at the proper time we will reap a harvest if we do not give up." The Bible teaches us to serve God through serving others. Instead of thinking about a year, let's break it down into smaller parts. How many months in a year? (12). How many weeks in a year? (52). How many days are in a year? (365). With all this time let us think about ways we can serve Jesus in the coming year. Do you have any ideas?

    Jesus' baptism marked the beginning of his ministry. Our baptism marks the beginning of our new life in Jesus. . Scripture: When all the people were being baptized, Jesus was baptized too. And as he was praying, heaven was opened and the Holy Spirit descended on him in bodily form like a dove. And a voice came from heaven: "You are my Son whom I love; with you I am well pleased." Luke 3:21-22 (NIV)

    This is an exciting time. It is the beginning of a brand new year. Some people like to make New Year's resolutions or promises to themselves about what they plan to accomplish in the new year. The number one resolution that people make is, "I am going to lose weight." I don't think too many people succeed, since it seems to be the number one resolution year after year. I know that it usually makes my top ten list of things I would like to accomplish in the new year.

Even if you don't make any New Year's resolutions, this is an exciting time. It is a time that we can forget our past mistakes and look forward to new opportunities that lie ahead of us. It is a time of new beginnings. Jesus experienced times of new beginnings in his life too. One of those times was when he was baptized. There were a couple of very important things that happened when Jesus was baptized.

First of all, the Bible tells us that the heavens opened and the Holy Spirit came down in the form of a dove and landed upon him. The second thing was that God spoke and said, "You are my Son. I love you and I am well-pleased with you." This event marked the beginning of Jesus' ministry here on earth. Up until that time, he had not performed any miracles, but with God's stamp of approval and with the spirit of God upon him, Jesus began to perform great miracles.

From this new beginning, many people began to understand that Jesus was truly the Son of God and they began to follow him. Our own baptism represents a new beginning for us as well. When we are baptized, it shows the world that just as Jesus rose from the dead through the glory of God the Father, we also live a new life in him. (Romans 6:4) God may not always be well-pleased with us, but I think that He looks down with an approving smile when he sees us trying to walk with Jesus.

New beginnings -- God gives us opportunities for new beginnings. Let us make the most of them as we live a new life in Christ through the power of his Holy Spirit. Proverbs 31 passage.8 read Proverbs 31:1-31 1. God's life does not change. 2. God's character does not change. 3. God's truth does not change. 4. God's ways do not change. 5. God's purposes do not change. 6. God's Son does not change.

We are the ones that change, some of us change by the people we are around, we allow them to mold us, change us in away we are more fun to be around, they don't have to change to be around us.. the way it should be. As a Christian we are changed into a vessel of the Holy Spirit, He dwells in us 24 7..not just a few seconds of the day when we are at church, ..we take Him home with us, we have him sit on the couch beside us, He sits at our meals and hears our prayers of thanksgiving to His Father in Heaven..and He also hears when we don't.

He sees who and what we bring into our homes, what do they say about this spirit that lives in your heart, what do your eyes watch, what do your ears hear, is Jesus smiling or is He sitting beside you with His head in His hands, wondering if your words were true, WHY are you making Him be crucified again with this sin. you say you love Him, you want to serve Him, that He is everything to you, but with your actions you take the whip and beat Him.

We are only a few days into the New Year, will you make this a new beginning for your true relationship with Jesus, a stronger one, a closer one, a more meaningful one.........HOW.. Prayer..talk to Him daily, greet the day with a thankful prayer, end it with praise. Ask Him to use you, place people in your path that are hurting that you can reach out to and share His love. Read your manual, really read it, any question you have. any trial you go through, any problem, pain, any problem has the answer in the Bible. once a month make it a job to do. go to shut in, a friend, a enemy and tell them how much they are loved, how answers can be found if you allow Jesus to hold it in His hands. write letters for people that write anymore, read to someone that cant read, do shopping for someone, there are so many things, when you think of others before you think of yourself.

Don't make a resolution, make a promise, a vow to be a better person to someone else, use this new year as a new beginning for yourself, to be a vessel, to hold the Spirit of our living God, to be poured out on all those around you .

Dear Father, thank you for new beginnings. Help us to make the most of them -- not through our own strength -- but through the power of the Holy Spirit that dwells within us. Amen.

Just short thoughts or prayers for situations in my life that may touch someone else, so many times we feel so alone in what our lives are unfolding. we cant change things and have to watch and learn from these things. what I am praying will happen, if something I go though may in some small way help someone going through the same thing ..just know your not alone, someone knows how you feel and what emotions are going through you. I wish so much to share the word with you and help you to see and understand, as a creation of God, changed by His grace and his love for us, NOTHING goes on in our life that hasn't passed through His hands first. He knows we can handle this and He will be with us and He will get the glory from this as we become stronger in His ways. I claim this and I stand on this now and always. Love and prayers to all

    Never be ashamed of the scars that life has left you with, A scar means the hurt is over, the wound is closed, you endured the pain and God has healed you.............you know when I saw this as a post on my face book page, I really started to think about what it said.

    Some times we think of the situation that made the scar, and think.. man that's a ugly thing...yes ugly things make scars, bad things make scars, but as the wound heals the pain is remembered less and less.

    When my children were born the pain was really bad, I refused pain killers for the health and love of my babies. but as soon as they were born the pain wasn't as bad any more. and over time it was forgotten.

    Same is the pain that has made the scars in your life. So many times in life we have to go through things to grow, painful at the time we go through them but as we heal we get stronger, have you ever really looked at a scar, it thicker skin, stronger than it was before.

    That is how you are inside when you make it through a situation that at the time seems to big, but you stand firm, plant your feet and keep saying to yourself..I know this is big God and I know I will be stronger from this. you WILLLL get the glory from this, give me the strength and wisdom to get through it and learn from this and be the person that can help someone else that I may come across later in life going through what I am right now.

    A few times in my life I have been very abused from the man in my life, my husbands, one was emotional, one was verbal and one physical. in all of them the emotional was the hardest to get over, the pain from the others went away, but it seemed emotional ones left the deepest scars.

    The emotional ones hurt the heart, self worth, self respect, and left a scar that went into my other relationships. a fear, lack of trust,it really made it hard to love anyone.

(But God)

I was able to find a man in church that knew the pain as I had, he had been the one hurt and he and I were able to grow together and help heal each other from our lessons learned. I was able to reach out to girl that was raped by being able to say I know how you are feeling, I have been there, I have been able to give God the glory for the pain by reaching out to others that are going through the things I had to grow through.

When you are able to look in there eyes and say I know how you feel and they know you really do understand because you went through it too, you can reach a person no one else can.

God will make a way when there seems no way. open a door when there doesn't seem to be one,if we leave the situation in His hands and listen when He speaks to your heart.

Don't let the pain turn you into something ugly, allow the pain to make you a creation God can use to help others. in that God will get the glory.

GOD OR MEDICINE

AMOXICILLIN How It Is Made

The preparation of amoxicillin involves a complex series of reactions that begins with penicillin produced by molds or other microorganisms. A variety of chemical reagents is then used to replace one hydrogen atom in the penicillin molecule by the $CH(NH_2)C_6H_4OH$ group that converts penicillin into amoxicillin.

Scottish bacteriologist Alexander Fleming (1881–1955) discovered penicillin in 1928. The antibiotic was first produced for human use in the early 1940s. Over time, researchers discovered ways of changing the chemical structure of penicillin to create semi-synthetic versions. The new antibiotics they created were more effective than penicillin against a wider range of bacteria, often with fewer side-effects. Amoxicillin was discovered by researchers at the Beecham pharmaceutical laboratories in 1962 and marketed about a decade later under the trade name of Amoxil®. The drug is now available under a number of trade names, including Larotid®, Trimox®, Wymox®, Polymox®, and Augmentin®.

You may be wondering what in the world is this one going to be about, you know its sort of funny how God just pops things in my head, but since the first part of Dec I have been sick off and on.

a few times after having hands laid on me the swelling and sore throat just went away by the time church was over, then a new germ would surface in the way of new illness.

This last time it was a really bad abscessed wisdom tooth, I was so close to emergency room visit but them what could they do really, they couldn't pull it out, so at 2am got online and found my Pastor was on line at that time too, so asked for prayer.

that pain went away but knew I needed medicine for the infection to heal enough to have it pulled, woke up so congested and had real bad cough, called Dr and then got some amoxicillin, today I woke up feeling so much better, I said a big thank you Jesus. but know some people will just say it was the meds..well think about this..

There are always going to be people that will try to talk there way into making you think there isn't a God, but for all of us that do its so easy to see HIM in all of it.

Mark 2; 1-12 Luke 5:17-26

The Great Physician:

Jesus referred to himself as physician twice:

Luke 4:23: And He said to them, "No doubt you will quote this proverb to Me, 'Physician, heal yourself!" Matt. 9:12-13: But when He heard this, He said, "It is not those who are healthy who need a physician, but those who are sick. But go and learn what this means, I desire compassion, and not sacrifice, for I did not come to call the righteous but sinners."

    I also started searching for information, this is what all I found;

The word used for physician in Greek was iatros, derived from iaomai, which refers to spiritual as well as physical healing (similar to the concept of shalom or rapha). Jesus was undoubtedly using the word "physician" to refer both to the spiritual and physical aspects of healing that He commanded.

A. Jesus' healing ministry was connected and related to his spiritual ministry. The paralytic, the woman with the hemorrhage, and the man born with MD all exhibited some degree of spiritual healing as well as physical healing.

B. Jesus used physical healing to exhibit His spiritual authority. He spiritually healed the paralytic first and then physically healed him to prove His power in the spiritual realm.

C. Jesus physically healed in order to glorify God. He healed the man who was born blind as a testimony to God's power, and He used it to draw the man unto Himself and to give testimony of God's power to the crowds as well as the Pharisees

D. Jesus healed out of compassion. Considering the hunger of Jairus' daughter shows Jesus' compassionate care for all of our needs. The feeding of the 5000 shows His desire to heal and feed the multitudes solely because of compassion.

E. Faith was an integral part of healing. In most cases, the person with the disease exhibited the faith. In one case, the faith was that of the father, and in one case the faith included that of two friends who brought the paralytic to Jesus. We can go even deeper from these verses that we must exhibit faith in God's healing power to be healed.

F. Healing was not necessarily a one-time event, but a process. Jesus proclaimed that He had healed the woman with the hemorrhage. The word used examples of spiritual as well as physical healing. Her physical healing was an outward sign of the work He had done in her heart. Then He told her to go in peace and be healed of her affliction. He had begun the work in her heart, but there was much work to be done. Furthermore, a great social healing needed to still occur because the woman would have been ostracized for 12 years for being ritually unclean. This example reminds us of the holistic nature of Jesus' ministry.

How can we apply these lessons to our lives and our family and friends?

A. We must remember that physical healing is not an end unto itself. Regardless of how well we do our jobs, people will eventually die. God may use us to exhibit some of His common grace, but its purpose is to draw them closer to Him, allowing for spiritual healing. We should regard physical healing as a way to give glory to God and to exhibit that He has power to heal spiritually as well.

B. God calls us to have compassion for people. This type of love can only occur through His work in us, and His love manifested through us. We are just too selfish on our own. But He desires to show compassion for the suffering by working through us. We are His hands and feet. Therefore, just as Jesus showed compassion for the sick, God calls us to do the same through His strength.

C. We must remember that shalom-type healing is a process. People just don't become whole overnight. God slowly works to break them and rebuild them when they are ready. We must realize this in our own lives as well as remembering that our ministry to our patients is a slow process, and their needs become different as they grow in the Lord.

D. We must glorify God when He uses us to heal. Never forget our commission, to glorify God in whatever we do (1 Cor. 10:31). As Jesus glorified God through healing, so should we. We must never take the credit. Whether God uses an antibiotic that we prescribed or a miracle to heal someone, He is still the healer, not us. Remember that.

Matt. 9:35-10:15: Jesus, seeing the multitudes, felt compassion for them, because they were distressed and downcast like sheep without a shepherd. He told them to pray for God to send out workers, and then proceeded to send the disciples themselves out.

Matt. 10.1: He gave them authority to cast out unclean spirits and to heal every kind of disease.

Matt. 10:7-8: He commanded them to preach, heal the sick, raise the dead, cleanse lepers, and cast out demons.

Matt. 10:9-10: He commanded them not to take anything with them or acquire money or supplies for their services, but to give freely what Jesus had given them. They were to stay with whoever accepted them, for a worker is worthy of his support (nourishment).

Luke 22:35-36: Jesus told the disciples that they could now to take a purse and bag with them, but He did not take away from His commission to preach and heal.

These verses give specific instructions for the disciples, including the command to(preach and heal.) He also instructed them that they were not to take extra possessions or charge for their services. But this was a short-term mission trip. Did Jesus mean for these instructions to continue long-term and be extended to other believers?

In a way we are all physicians , we have that same healing power that Jesus had in the palm of our hands, when we place our hands on someone and pray, or ask healing over the phone or even over the computer through chat lines, those lines go straight to God, in turn God sends His healing through you to where it needs to go.

Jesus us told us to go out and heal the sick in His name that the Father in Heaven be glorified, we have our patients around us everyday, family, friends, strangers by you in the store.

You see them in the row with medicine, you know they aren't feeling good, pray. you see someone in the cold outside coughing, pray..you hold your grand baby and feel it wheezing pray. its all in the power of your spoken word and faith, with out faith your just breathing air in and out, it means nothing and that's what you will get in return. FAITH that's what its all about.

now its up to you, God or Medicine, it should always be Thank YOU JESUS

"*FAITH AND UNSEEN ILLNESSES*"
HOW THEY CAN BE THE SAME

"*HAB 2:4 MATT 8:10 MATT 9:22 MATT 17:20*"
ROM 1:17 ROM 10:17 GAL 5:6
1 THES 5:8 HEB 11:1 JAMES 2:20

    You may be wondering what this could be about, and its the connection of things unseen, things you just have to know are real even though you can't see it. Over the past few years there have been things changing in my friends, family, and in me personally.

    When you see someone that has a mental problem, let's say just being a little slow, or maybe the first signs of Alzheimer's, maybe a little bit autistic, or has something like fibromyalgia, or other things you just can't see with the eyes.

    When I was told I had Fibromyalgia it was really hard and sometimes it still can be, when you go for a job and when they ask if you have any reason you may not be able to do a part of this job and you explain. they cant see it. But you know you will have limits and they will just see it as being lazy.

    When you have a learning problem and you are doing your best to be normal and really just don't want to wear a sign around your neck saying I have trouble reading, its hard for me to understand directions.

    This has really been hard to deal with in my own life, there are so many things I wish I could still do, I would love to be able to still do in-home care, but cant do stairs because of arthritis, and now if I strain any muscles the fibromyalgia will cause very deep, burning in my body and it will just sort of move around.

    Sometimes if I can't do things the way I used to, it may appear I just don't want to, just don't want to go anyplace or do anything, they can't see that it's because I know it will cause 2 days of pain. They can't see it.

    When you have a learning problem and you just can't understand something, or just can't read what it says, some people will get mad, call you names, make fun of you and say very mean things, like if you can't do the work why not just get out of here.

    They see a lazy person, where really what it is was is the fact you have to take your time to do the same things they may be able to do a lot faster, but *for them it's very hard to put things together, or put things back where they belong because they can't read the label.*

True friends are the ones that may not see your illness but are there to help you with it, help you to do things in a way it wont hurt you or cause you to be embarrassed in front of others.

They know doing something is going to hurt you so they ask if they can help you, they don't see your illness but they know its real, they know you wouldn't make it up and they trust you even if they may not be able to see it.

Well now I am going to relate this to another problem some may have with their vision problems, faith of the unseen,the unknown, things that are really there but we can't see them. Like sitting on chair that you can't see.

My pastor uses this sometimes, it's easy to sit in a chair you can see when some one tells you to sit, but what if they told you to sit and you couldn't see the chair, would you still go sit down.

In Hab 2:4 Behold, the soul of him is lifted up, *and* is not upright; but the just shall live by his faith. Those that expect to hear from God must withdraw from the world, and get above it, There are some who will proudly "disregard this vision, "whose hearts are so lifted up that they scorn to take notice of it; if God will work for them immediately, they will thank him, but they will not give him credit; their hearts are lifted up towards vanity, and, since God puts them off, they will shift for themselves and not be beholden to him; they think *their own hands sufficient for them*, and God's promise is to them an insignificant thing. That man's soul that is thus *lifted up is not upright in him;* it is not right with God, is not as it should be. Those that either distrust or despise God's all-sufficiency will not walk uprightly with him, <u>Gen 17:1</u>. But, (2.) Those who are truly good, and whose hearts are upright with God, will value the promise, and venture their all upon it; and, in confidence of the truth of it, will keep close to God and duty in the most difficult

The just shall live by faith; during the captivity good people shall support themselves, and live comfortably, by faith in these precious promises, while the performance of them is deferred. *The just shall live by his faith,* by that faith which he acts upon the word of God. This is quoted in the New Testament (<u>Rom 1:17</u>; <u>Gal 3:11</u>;

Heb 10:38), for the proof of the great doctrine of justification by faith only and of the influence which the grace of faith has upon the Christian life. Those that are made *just by faith shall live,* shall be happy here and for ever; while they are here, they live by it; when they come to heaven faith shall be swallowed up in vision.

There will be some people that will only see part of a vision because they don't have that faith to wait on God's will, they get part of the vision and say OK that's it, I know this is what God want's me to go and they jump into something before God had all the path laid out for them.

Oh how many times I have done this, to wait is to have faith, the reason doors close is before the path was there you took off running, like a man on a horse that knows it wants to run and he kicks to make her go.

The horse knew the way but the rider gets knocked off cause he didn't know where to duck the limbs, the limbs of life so to say, yes God may have said run, but if you had sat and let Him finish He would have said, let me go prepare your way.

Matt 8:10..well go on and read to 13. in this we see a man that had to have the faith strong enough for the healing of his son

from Henry commentary; Note, God has his remnant among all sorts of people. No man's calling or place in the world will be an excuse for his unbelief and impiety; none shall say in the great day, I had been religious, if I had not been a soldier; for such there are among the *ransomed of the Lord.* And sometimes where grace conquers the unlikely, it is more than a conqueror; this soldier that was good, was very good. (2.) Though he was a Roman soldier, and his very dwelling among the Jews was a badge of their subjection to the Roman yoke, yet Christ, who was *King of the Jews,* favored him; and therein has taught us to do good to our enemies, and not needlessly to interest ourselves in national enmities.

You know sometimes I think we are to have faith so strong that He can lead us to go to the very person that we may think of like a enemy, that person may have the piece of the puzzle you were looking for, we have to have a humble heart and not feel"they don't have anything I need" I can do this all by myself. And that's where you end up, by yourself.

When God tells us to speak to someone,go to someone, reach out to someone that may be hurting and you don"t have that faith to step out and know God will now go before me and prepare the way, He will give me the words and the actions and I wont speak unless I know its His words.

When we need a healing, we have to have that faith to know if we pray and ask God to heal us or a family member we have to hold fast to KNOWING if it is God's time and His will it will be so.

But they may have a lesson they have to learn too, for the healing to manifest in them or us. In my life this has happened, when the Dr told me the things I had going on, I went home prayed and just waited for the pain to go away and never come back..and waited..and waited, Ok Jesus I believe whats up ???

Then a friend came to me, in pain the same pain, Oh wow I know what that feels like, I knew what it feels like when your skin hurts to be touched, when you get upset about something you don't just feel upset, now your nerve endings flair up and your pain is worse.

And if you get very upset, you not only hurt, now you sometimes get hives along with it, Fibromyalgia isn't a illness you can see, but it's there, so very real but only you know that for a fact.

Mat 9:21 **For she said within herself, If only I shall touch His robe, I will be whole.**

Mat 9:22 **But turning and seeing her, Jesus said, Daughter, be comforted; your faith has saved you. And the woman was saved from that hour.**

So why do some of us have to suffer with this and also things like arthritis,osteoarthritis, things that hurt so bad,well what I have done is use the pain to understand others that have pain, to have real compassion because of having understanding of it all.

Sometimes it may be God knows who He wants to use in different areas because He made you, He knows your spirit, He knows you can handle something in order to reach out to someone else that may not be able to handle it.

Am I being a martyr no, all I am saying even when your body may not be in perfect condition God can still use you, I may hurt but I am not going to just sit in self pity cause I know I have a job to do. And God is my new boss.

People that have learning disabilities, but not so much they can't be used, they can help others with disabilities to know they are NOT worthless in any way shape or form, they were created the very same way you were.

You help them find something they are really good at and build around that, some people that may not be able to read can get a computer that has a audio speaker built in, and can follow along when it reads out loud.

They learn things that they can do and do it well , as you all know My husband has this issue and has learned so much from his computer, he can fix most things on our cars from being able to watch and learn from videos.

He could have sat back and just let it go and give up but he never gave up and he is reaching out in different ministries in our apartment complex and at church, we have to allow God to reach them and then we can show them how to develop there ideas and goals.

We look at some people and wonder how they can be so up and glorify God when going through the things they do, as with a woman the was paralyze at 16 from the neck down, did she give up, NO she is now leader and speaker for others with disabilities and in wheel chairs. She uses the rest of her body, to write and paint with her mouth.

She held tight to knowing nothing happens that doesn't go through God's hands first, she has gone through so many things and is such a inspiration for me and I keep up with her work and new things on line even now.

There is no disability so big God can't use you if your heart is willing. Mat 17:20 And Jesus said to them, Because of your unbelief. For truly I say to you, If you have faith like a grain of mustard seed, you shall say to this mountain, Move from here to there. And it shall move. And nothing shall be impossible to you.

Matthew Henry commentary;

They came to Jesus apart. Note, Ministers, who are to deal for Christ in public, have need to keep up a private communion with him, that they may in secret, where no eye sees, bewail their weakness and straightness, their follies and infirmities, in their public performances, and enquirer into the cause of them. We should make use of the liberty of access we have to Jesus apart, where we may be free and particular with him. Such questions as the disciples put to Christ, we should put to ourselves, in communing with our own hearts upon our beds; Why were we so dull and careless at such a time? Why came we so much short in such a duty? That which is amiss may, when found out, be amended.

2. Christ gives them two reasons why they failed.

(1.) It was *because of their unbelief,* Mat 17:20. When he spake to the father of the child and to the people, he charged it upon their unbelief; when he spake to his disciples, he charged it upon theirs; for the truth was, there were faults on both sides; but we are more concerned to hear of our own faults than of other people's, and to impute what is amiss to ourselves than to others. When the preaching of the word seems not to be so successful as sometimes it has been, the people are apt to lay all the fault upon the ministers, and the ministers upon the people; whereas, it is more becoming for each to own his own faultiness, and to say, "It is owing to me." Ministers, in reproving, must learn thus to give to each his portion of the word; and to take people off from judging others, by teaching all to judge themselves; *It is because of your unbelief.* Though they had faith, yet that faith was weak and ineffectual. Note, [1.] As far as faith falls short of its due strength, vigor, and activity, it may truly be said, "There is unbelief." Many are chargeable with unbelief, who yet are not to be called *unbelievers.* [2.] It is because of our unbelief, that we bring so little to pass in religion, and so often miscarry, and come short, in that which is good.

Our Lord Jesus takes this occasion to show them the power of faith, that they might not be defective in that, another time, as they were now; *If ye have faith as a grain of mustard-seed,* ye shall do wonders, Mat 17:20. Some make the comparison to refer to the quality of the mustard-seed, which is, when bruised, sharp and penetrating; "If you have an active growing faith, not dead, flat, or insipid, you will not be baffled thus." But it rather refers to the quantity; "If you had but a grain of true faith, though so little that it were like that which is the least of all seeds, you would do wonders." Faith in general is a firm assent to, a compliance with, and a confidence in, all divine revelation. The faith here required, is that which had for its object that particular revelation by which Christ gave his disciples power to work miracles in his name, for the confirmation of the doctrine they preached.

I went out and got some mustard seeds awhile back for my kids class, those things are so tiny, as I studied them and got the lesson ready, I got to thinking, so many times these young ones are so trusting.

If mommy or daddy tell them something its true,(look at Santa and the Easter bunny) but the point is God said to come with a child like spirit to Him, why do you think He said that? Because if we did, when He told us something we would trust, without seeing, we would have faith that all He said was true, no doubts. God does not lie to us, God doesn't want harm to come to us, God will not put us in danger, God will not lead us to sin.

If anytime you are getting ready to do something you, stop. Wait.

Pray. And allow God to lead you, things will go smooth for you, you can't jump ahead of His will, and you will know very fast if you have. Some other scriptures you may want to check out are listed above, they all speak of faith, believing without seeing, that one is **Heb 11:1** *Now faith is the substance of things hoped for, the evidence of things not seen.*

Just because you may not see something does not mean it isn't real or isn't really there, look through God's eyes, and feel with God's love, be open to His will and don't rush Him, wait on Him and listen when He speaks.

Oh Jesus I know your real, I don't see you but I know your here, I can't hear your voice but You speak to me, I may not have the healing I want in the flesh, but know my heart, mind and spirit are yours and someday when I am in heaven with You I will have that perfect body with not a pain in sight.

For now I don't care about the pain I feel once in awhile, its nothing compared to the suffering You did for me on the cross, mine is nothing, your suffering was the big one, my time on this earth is to be your servant.

As long as I have breath and can go, can type, can speak, can smile, and hold my husband, children, give hugs, and hold babies, I am yours, the joy I feel in all of that is my joy, my peace, and as I sit with tears of joy in my eyes, listening to "How Great Is Our God" I give you praise and love you with all my heart.

So what you may wonder could have been so bad in my life that I didn't feel God could just forgive me, In my mind it was so big, but I have come to know that no matter what we have done in the past, His graces covers it all.

I had a very bad habit of always wanting to help people when they were hurting, maybe trying to make amends for my earlier years in a way, the men I had in my life always needed something.

One was getting over the death of his father, lost the love of his life to another man, me to the rescue. Then one who had his girl he just got engaged to be murdered where she worked, then a man that had never been married and a loner, I just knew I could be the one to fix them.

All I did was end up getting hurt because I fell in love, married 4 of them all to find I couldn't fix the problems or replace the ones they had lost, and when the marriage fell apart it was so easy to see what it was.

I had made it so easy to fall into my arms and have sex to make it all go way that it's all they had in mind. And then the man that always came around from the time I was in high school.

He really had it easy, he knew he was almost my first love, any time I went through a break up or divorce he was there to pick up the pieces, in 1974,1985,1990,1993 and I always went into his arms for my comfort.

But after being called into the ministry it all changed, in 1996 my life really turned around, I had been seeing him again as a friend and when I got my divorce he wanted to pick up the pieces again.

But I realized something, he was looking for a woman to fill the empty spot he had that only Jesus could fill, I left a note for him and shared that with him, I then lost the building he was allowing me to use for my bible studies and also my job as gardener at Lake.

When I turned him down it hurt him pretty bad and then when I started seeing the man that would be my next mission and husband it hurt him more because he felt he was so much better than him.

He was homeless, and wanted to learn all about my ministry and his lies began, he had studied me for weeks and knew just how to make me believe him and think this poor baby needed someone to give him a chance in life.

Well he was a con artist, but I didn't see it at that point, I was married to that man for 10 years that took the very life out of me, I am not even going to give him the glory of writing down all the pain he caused me in my life and my children.

Only that I know God never took His eyes off me for a second and He had his angels around me working double shifts for those 10 awful years, but they were years of finding out something I never knew about me.

I was a survivor, and had lived to share it with others that maybe just maybe they have gone through some of the same things I have, and in that my pain, my lessons, my broken heart, have all been blessings under cover. The thing I say now is when things aren't going good, it's like no worries. I know God will get the glory some way through this.

I was homeless for 7 months, and learned how to take wet twigs and make a fire, to fish for food, wash clothes on rocks and be a real girl scout to survive and not be afraid of the dark but to feel safe when all alone with just 2 dogs and a cat because my husband was being held in jail for a few weeks.

God has always been by my side, even when at times I know it broke His heart to see the things I was doing and taking part in, some things I know he helped heal the pain of the memories from things I was made to do for a very sick husband just to make his ego feel good, he always wanted attention and would want things to shock people if we got caught in the act in public places.

So thankful God protected me in those times by keeping the sickness from anyone's eyes, the shame would make me sick to my stomach and make him laugh and go get high. The power over me made him feel like a man.

The memories these things have left may be a scar but it's a healed pain, the scar means the wound is healed over and in time the scar will also go away, when I am able to help someone that is going through this pain in her life my scar will be gone.

I work at tour home from 1806, *I love giving tours and sharing what I know about the house, people and town and feel like they got their money's worth.*

  I know there are some places you don't feel like they could care less and I really do care, I love this house, my job and meeting new people, and love dressing up in these old clothes, love the long skirts and bonnets, its just so me.

  Sometimes I almost feel like I was born at another time and reliving this area. It just feels so normal for me and gives me a feeling of being home comfort just can't be explained.

  You know in school I didn't like history at all and since working at this old house, I just love it, can't seem to learn enough about the town, its people, what went on in the 1800s.

  There was so much I also learned at old farm house I used to rent in the late 90s, it was built in the year 1858, and it had a feel to it, like it had a story to tell, I went to town one day and went to the assessor's office.

  Come to find out it had been a safe house for free slaves, they were being hunted down by people that didn't want them free, when I found that out I started checking the house out, they would have had some sort of hiding place.

  After checking the basement I was looking at the walls, in the bedroom there was a place that looked different, the paneling had a seam down it and saw mark at the bottom.

  Very carefully I pried the floor board away and the framing at the top and pulled it away, inside there was a place for two benches, little cubby holes, a tin cup, camping type plate of tin, two very old dresses with a bonnet.

  I took the dresses out and the bonnet and hung them on my walls, they rest I didn't touch, just left it the way it was, a memory to cherish, that house had a few other little things, things I didn't share with just anyone.

  Once when feeding my animals in the barns, my dogs started acting funny, just sitting and whimpering, I looked out the door from the ledge of step. It was up higher than the rest of door.

  As I looked I could hear kids playing and giggling, I saw the grass weeds being mashed like they were playing ring around the rosy, the two dogs were sitting there watching also. I talked to the dogs and it stopped, I called a friend Carrie the next day that could see spirits and know if they were ok and made appointment for her to come out and so now I waited and didn't say anything to anyone.

She came out the next day and walked around the house, barn and yard, she said there were spirits of children all over the place, not harming but feeling comfort, it was as if they claimed me as the mother and found comfort in being around me.

There was such peace in that I never felt afraid again. I know there are some people that feel any spirit that dies isn't able to be around only demons, but I don't feel like that, I think there are ones that are afraid to leave where they felt safe and I think there are also some that say if their spouses are left behind and they want to wait for them.

I do not feel all spirit are bad, I know there are some to fear and the devil has some out there, but I also know God is stronger than any of them I just the name of Jesus brings them to their knees.

There was a time I felt the evil ones, at a friend's home when away from the spirit of God and going the wrong way, it was in the late 80s and my drinking and party days.

I was going out with some friends and got very drunk, they were my family in my drunk state and I loved them so much, but they were very evil, they saw a person they could control.

That night after bar hopping all night we went back to their trailer, they gave me more to drink and we smoked a little pot, they explained how the husband couldn't be satisfied with just one woman, and if he was to have someone else it would be easier for the wife if it was me.

That she would be there to, I would be safe, so all three of us were in bed and it's like I was out of my body watching, it wasn't me, this went on for hours and the next day I could remember little pieces but not sure if I dreamed it or it was real, I found out later that it was very real and now they were coming to me alone to see if I would have sex with them one on one. I said no, it was to help them together not alone.

That evening I saw dark shadows move across the room, it was over and over again, she asked if I saw them and I said yes, she said we see them a lot after we go to bed, they float around the room, yes I think it was demons and they lived in that house.

When they kept coming to me I ended the friendship with both of them, I saw them as just wanting to be a playmate, not help them in their marriage, I was so stupid and was so trusting.

I haven't seen them again since, there were so many things in my life I regret, things that I am so ashamed of, even knowing God forgives me it's so hard to forgive myself.

They had also introduced me to a biker guy from St Louis, he was looking for a nice girl to date not like the ones in the area he lived, they wanted me to meet him,(this was before the other thing I just wrote about) they set up phone numbers and for about a month or so we talked on the phone everyday, I was separated from my husband but wasn't divorced yet so really didn't feel right about seeing him yet, so when the divorce was done, I went out to their house to meet this man.

We had meal, talked and drank and drank some more, I am not one to drink very much at all and they got me a bottle of Hot-Dam, a drink that tasted like red hots, loved it and drank it down pretty fast.

I don't remember leaving their house, I don't remember playing pool and doing really good, I don't remember going home to their house, all I do remember is waking up next to a man I had just met.

The thought that went through my head was I am no better than the sluts he had talked about that he didn't want anything to do with, I slipped out of bed got dressed and went home .

I was so ashamed I got in the shower trying to wash my guilt away in tears, after I got dressed my friend called me and I told her how I felt, she said they had also been talking and he liked me, they knew it was the alcohol and not me.

They talked me into coming back out there and we had a long talk, he had told me he was feeling guilty for taking advantage of me and if I could forgive him he would like to keep dating and we did for awhile.

I helped put his Harley back together when he had worked on it 16 hours straight, nothing was working right in getting the clutch back together, I had watched very close to everything he did so I said, can I try?

I just reversed what he had done when he took it apart, when he saw what I was doing he was so amazed, he said well I will go take it for a ride and see how you did.

He was gone about 20 minutes and had a smile from ear to ear, said it was working better than before, picked me up and was swinging me around, I loved being able to help.

But in no way was I a biker woman material and after 6 months we decided it was not a life to raise three children, it was way to dangerous for me and them, we split up and stayed friends.

Sometimes I wonder if that is why it's so hard for me to say no to helping people now, does a part of me feel like If I do enough good it will cover all the bad, will it make it go away in my head.

THE HOLINESS OF GOD

What does it mean to be Holy, there are so many ways it is spoke about in the bible, and so many ways we hear pastors preach on it, but does it really mean.

Websters:

Holy

HO'LY, a.

1. Properly, whole, entire or perfect, in a moral sense. Hence, pure in heart, temper or dispositions; free from sin and sinful affections. Applied to the Supreme Being, holy signifies perfectly pure, immaculate and complete in moral character; and man is more or less holy, as his heart is more or less sanctified, or purified from evil dispositions. We call a man holy,when his heart is conformed in some degree to the image of God, and his life is regulated by the divine precepts. Hence, holy is used as nearly synonymous with good, pious, godly.

Be ye holy; for I am holy. 1 Pet 1.

2. Hallowed; consecrated or set apart to a sacred use, or to the service or worship of God; a sense frequent in Scripture; as the holy sabbath; holy oil; holy vessels; a holy nation; the holy temple; a holy priesthood.

3. Proceeding from pious principles,or directed to pious purposes; as holy zeal.

4. Perfectly just and good; as the holy law of God.

5. Sacred; as a holy witness.

Holy of Holiest, in Scripture, the innermost apartment of the Jewish tabernacle or temple, where the ark was kept,and where no person entered, except the high priest, once a year.

Holy Ghost, or Holy Spirit, the Divine Spirit; the third person in the Trinity;

the sanctifying of souls.

Holy war, a war undertaken to rescue the holy land, the ancient Judea, from the infidels; a crusade; an expedition carried on by Christians against the Saracens in the eleventh, twelfth and thirteenth centuries; a war carried on in a most unholy manner.

There are so many ways we hear it used, Ex 3:5 the place where Moses stood was holy ground. Ex 20:8 to keep the sabbath day holy,...Deut 7:6

Deu 7:6 Do this because you are a people set apart as holy to GOD, your God. GOD, your God, chose you out of all the people on Earth for himself as a cherished, personal treasure.

The question is .. would we know holiness if it touched our face, if it stood in front of us ..if we heard the voice. If we are to know it if we see it ,we first have to know what it is.

Over the past few months I have been listening to a station called JoyFm, its a all christian station with beautiful praise music 24 hours a day. the song "What do I know of Holy" was playing and it touched my spirit so very much.

The question came into me on a personal level, what did I know of holy.

The search was then started, it was so strange as I searched so many things had new meaning to me, As I searched God started showing me in so many new ways.

praise music would so many times bring tears to my eyes for there beauty, but now they bring tears because they touch my soul.

What did I know of Holy?? ..not as much as I thought.

You see if you learn what holy is you can then understand how deeply Gods love for you really is, it is more personal.

In the verse in Deut we are made holy because He is holy, when you have Jesus in your heart you become a Holy vessel to God , A temple for His presence to live.

Act 1:8 What you'll get is the Holy Spirit. And when the Holy Spirit comes on you, you will be able to be my witnesses in Jerusalem, all over Judea and Samaria, even to the ends of the world."

We will have the words to say in all places we may go ..we are Holy vessels, there is no need to fear, because the words that come from us wont be our own.

Rom 12:1 *So here's what I want you to do, God helping you: Take your everyday, ordinary life--your sleeping, eating, going-to-work, and walking-around life--and place it before God as an offering. Embracing what God does for you is the best thing you can do for him.*

In everything we do, do it as if you are doing it for God, think of it as a gift from God you are able to do your job, to have food to eat, to go for walks and enjoy the world he created, feel Him around you in all of it.

1Co 6:19 *Or didn't you realize that your body is a sacred place, the place of the Holy Spirit? Don't you see that you can't live however you please, squandering what God paid such a high price for? The physical part of you is not some piece of property belonging to the spiritual part of you.*

Keep yourself healthy as you can, watch what you put into your temple

1Pe 1:15 *As obedient children, let yourselves be pulled into a way of life shaped by God's life, a life energetic and blazing with holiness.*

1Pe 1:16 God said, "I am holy; you be holy."

we are so very special to God, He loves us so much, anyone that is a parent knows the love you feel for your child, and the hurt when they rebel, Gods love is so very much stronger and His desire for what he knows you can be brings so very much joy to Him.

As a child of God we are special,... chosen, ...set apart, ...sacred, .. a special treasure as Deut 7 :6 tells us. and we carry His presence in us, ..on us, through us, ..all around us, ..in the scriptures people were healed in the shadow of Holy men, the same thing is in you if you have the knowledge and belief to allow it to flow from you.

You know my mom always said Susan Kay, the only limits you have are the ones you place on yourself,

I think sometimes God is telling me the same thing, and He is telling each one of us.

Sometimes you hear of some people who have been in a accident where they lived and the person to save them stepped in front of them and passed away, they feel bad and ask why did they die, for me, how could they have loved me that much, but don't you see.

We all have someone that had that much love, so much that he died the most painful death any person could do for you, for me, and for your children and grandchildren that aren't even born yet.

That love never changes, never goes away,..What do you know of Holy. In the presence of the holy spirit you feel its warmth, you can feel love penetrate to your soul, when the anointing is around you it sometimes makes you feel weak.

But more than anything its the presence of the strongest love you will ever feel, a love that s unconditional, that's all forgiving, that's all comforting . It can bring you to tears or bring you to your knees.

What is Holy, to me it means so full of Gods love that it pours all over everyone around you and everything you touch, That God is your voice, your words,your actions and your thoughts. Are we Holy, maybe not yet but we are to strive daily to be as close as we can in this human body to be Christ like in all ways. This IS my desire and will be daily, from the time I awake till I fall asleep at night, let this be your desire and we can all make the world a wonderful place to be.

HOW GREAT IS OUR GOD

This has become so very real to me this past few weeks, You see we had allowed this cat to finish having her babies in our basement about the last week of may. it seemed like the right thing to do at the time. Little did I know things were about to change for us in a big way, a way we never thought about in a hundred years.

"BUT GOD" had so many other plans for us. Tom has a job through someplace called experience works, it helps find jobs for people 55 years old's and older, well they had to cut his hours because of government cuts. this meant less pay but same bills had to be paid. we knew the only thing we could do is start looking for another place to rent, in our search my sister told us about apt opening in senior area.

This would be perfect, on one floor and no steps. the papers went through without any problems...the first of July we could begin moving into our new home. I could take Izzie and my bird Obidiah...but no cats.....the babies... oh no. the search for homes was on. we found one we thought.(have sense found out he is girl bird Sunshine now)

But they called back and said they didn't have open cage, a friend said she would keep them a day or so..well this turned into from July 1st till the 18th with no homes we thought we were going to have to put them down, this broke our hearts..more phone calls, more no thanks, so desperate now, our prayers came with tears.

Sunday evening as I was in prayer the words filled my heart as if vocal. "I am not a God of Death, but a God of life"I was filled with such peace, then 7:30 am , a woman called with opening at Safe Harbor in Jackson, then about 15 minuets later a lady called wanting the little calico girl. homes for all the babies.

The feeling of God taking care of even His smallest creatures came into our hearts. as God cares for the sparrow he also watches over you. but then we got to Safe harbor, how great a God we have came into view, not only is it a no kill shelter, it was a animal paradise, lots of room,clean, medical staffing, and all ages together, play things beds..just perfect. God not only heard our prayers but went above and beyond to show His love for our animals and for blessing our hearts in the biggest way. Matt 10:29 Mat 10:29 "What's the price of a pet canary?

Some loose change, right? And God cares what happens to it even more than you do. we have to see God created every living creature and he loves them so much more than we could ever even try to. there was no way He would not hear all the prayers going out for these little kittens to find good homes Col 4:2 Pray diligently.

Stay alert, with your eyes wide open in gratitude. the children in the church and there mom asked prayers from our members to keep these little ones lifted up, we prayed with tears and concern. Luke 17:6 But the Master said, "You don't need more faith.

There is no 'more' or 'less' in faith. If you have a bare kernel of faith, say the size of a poppy seed, you could say to this sycamore tree, 'Go jump in the lake,' and it would do it. you know sometimes I think we put God in way to small of a box.

He will use the smallest of creatures to get your attention and make you think. and then this morning, I get so full of peace, I sit down at my desk to start study... there is a praying mantis in the curtain right above my laptop, a baby one..this isn't the first time this has happened, in 1998 one stayed above my desk for 3 day before it moved....ok God what is it you want me to know..what could this mean. when I came home from work 6 hours later it is still right above my laptop table..what is it what do you want me to hear from you at this time God ..

So I go on line and look up the insect...guess what Praying Mantis Meanings in the Animal Symbolism...The mantis comes to us when we need peace, quiet and calm in our lives. Usually the mantis makes an appearance when we've flooded our lives with so much business, activity, or chaos that we can no longer hear the still small voice within us because of the external din we've created. (wow does that ever hit this week of moving)

After observing this creature for any length of time you can see why the symbolism of the praying mantis deals with stillness and patience. The mantis takes her time, and lives her life at her own silent pace. A quick-list of praying mantis symbolism: Stillness Awareness Creativity Patience Mindful Calm Balance Intuition These traits have lead the mantis to be a symbol of meditation and contemplation.

In fact, in China, the mantis has long been honored for her mindful movements. The mantis never makes a move unless she is 100% positive it is the right thing for her to do. This is a message to us to contemplate and be sure our minds and souls all agree together about the choices we are making in our lives. Overwhelmingly in most cultures the mantis is a symbol of stillness.

As such, she is an ambassador from the animal kingdom giving testimony to the benefits of meditation, and calming our minds. An appearance from the mantis is a message to be still, go within, meditate, get quite and reach a place of calm.

It may also a sign for you to be more mindful of the choices you are making and confirm that these choices are congruent. --------------------- As I shared in one of my other studies, God has always used things to get my attention.

One time it was the butterfly, thousands, in the air, on my arms and legs, why.. I asked for a sign to know if this was the right time to go back to Missouri, why the butterfly, it was time for its migration as it was also mine, it was time for me to move on to safer place for the changes to be able to take place. the butterfly has a very special place in my heart because of this talk God had with me. the butterfly.

Butterfly Animal Symbolism Overwhelmingly, cultural myth and lore honor the butterfly as a symbol of transformation because of its impressive process of metamorphosis. From egg, to larvae (caterpillar), to pupa (the chrysalis or cocoon) and from the cocoon the butterfly emerges in her unfurling glory. What a massive amount of transition this tiny creature undergoes.

Consider for a moment the kind of energy this expends. I dare say if a human were to go through this kind of change we'd freak out! Imagine the whole of your life changing to such an extreme you are unrecognizable at the end of the transformation. Mind you, this change takes place in a short span of about a month too (that's how long the butterfly life cycle is). Herein lies the deepest symbolic lesson of the butterfly.

She asks us to accept the changes in our lives as casually as she does. The butterfly unquestioningly embraces the chances of her environment and her body. This unwavering acceptance of her metamorphosis is also symbolic of faith. Here the butterfly beckons us to keep our faith as we undergo transitions in our lives. She understands that our toiling, fretting and anger are useless against the turning tides of nature – she asks us to recognize the same.

A quick-list of Butterfly animal symbolism: Resurrection Transition Celebration Lightness Time Soul Interestingly, in many cultures the butterfly is associated with the soul – further linking our animal symbolism of faith with the butterfly. In Greek myth, Psyche (which literally translates to mean "soul") is represented in the form of a butterfly. Befittingly, Psyche is forever linked with love as she and Eros (the Greek god of love, also known in Roman myth as Cupid) shared an endlessly passionate bond together – both hopelessly in love with the other.

Greece doesn't corner the market on associating the butterfly with the soul. Here are a few other ancient cultures that associated this elegant creature with the soul: Asian (central) Mexican – Aztec New Zealand Zaire Even Christianity considers the butterfly a soulful symbol. To wit, the butterfly is depicted on ancient Christian tombs, as Christ has been illustrated holding a butterfly in Christian art.

It's connection with the soul is rather fitting. We are all on a long journey of the soul. On this journey we encounter endless turns, shifts, and conditions that cause us to morph into ever-finer beings. At our soul-journey's end we are inevitably changed – not at all the same as when we started on the path. To take this analogy a step further, we can look again to the grace and eloquence of the butterfly and realize that our journey is our only guarantee. Our responsibility to make our way in faith, accept the change that comes, and emerge from our transitions as brilliantly as the butterfly.

So now I think he is wanting to find my still place, a place for me to be still and know He is God, to never think He doesn't hear our every prayer, to trust Him with all that is in me and know His will is what will be and He will have the glory. there are reasons for everything that happens in our life, and sometimes,

God will use the smallest thing to tap into your heart. but you have to stay in close touch with Him to see it..to hear it..and to feel it. God created us to have all these senses to be able to use them. Oh thank you God for creating me with the mind and heart to want to keep reaching, keep learning, always wanting to do more to bring Glory to your precious name.

My life had purpose and meaning, Things really started to make since to me, all the whys I had in my life now had answers, the puzzle of my life had all the pieces now and I understood what I was to do and how.

But I had to learn a new lesson, how to pace myself, how to grow and also forgive myself, I knew God had forgiven me, but my past had a hold of me and I was going into battle daily with this issue, Feeling like I could never do enough to have forgiveness, feeling like I always had to do more to earn my forgiveness, till my body started having the effects from it.

This started out just being my journal, a place to write down my thoughts, fears, dreams and goals, I would write to Matilda every day, my name as a child from a very dear uncle, But what has happened is as I poured out to Matilda, I learned more about myself than I ever had, as I wrote and God spoke to my heart things I had never seen in my life took form.

I went on writing and as I did it went through my mind, this isn't just for me to hear, I knew there are others that have been in my shoes and some are in them now looking for their own answers.

I hope, I pray that anyone that picks this book up and reads it that God will speak to you as He did me and open your eyes to what He has taught me, may you all be blessed and go to share it with others.

Only then can you find out what can happen when your heart, mind

and spirit are one. Then God can mold you into a vessel to hold His glory, so full you pour out to everyone around you.

In 2011, I was told the pains I was having were do to so many things going on in my body, the test showed I was having osteoarthritis, osteoporosis, and by drawing I made of where this unusual moving pains were, I also was in beginning stages of Fibromyalgia.

In studying this I found that because of all the years of stress in my life, it was if my body was having a breakdown in the nerves, some people have mental breakdown, mine was in the body.

The past year I have been doing so many things in my ministry, jobs, learning new things for where I work, making things to ware and show how it was in the 1800s, I loved it, also teaching classes for women, children 7 websites, and 3 books in 2 years.

So this week when I woke up feeling like I was run over with a truck I asked myself whats happening, I am doing things to lose weight, watching what I am eating, on liquid diet due to getting 7 teeth pulled.

Well my sister made a list for me on what all was going on in my life, to see it written down was something I never did. Seeing the list made me see my plate was over flowing and change had to take place soon for the health of me.

I had worked so hard trying to earn my forgiveness that now from years of stress never feeling worthy or having love of self, never seeing myself as a forgiven vessel, I was now paying a very high price.

I think I have finally come to the place of letting it go, allowing God to take me day by day, fill my spirit with the love He has for me and allow me to reach out to others going through this, because now I am able to see it in others.

You can only feel others pain when you have really been there, you can say oh I know how you feel, but in reality you don't the the pain in their heart, their mind and their body till you have walked in their shoes.

DO YOU KNOW A LOST LAMB

Luk 15:4

"Suppose one of you had a hundred sheep and lost one. Wouldn't you leave the ninety-nine in the wilderness and go after the lost one until you found it?

Luk 15:5

When found, you can be sure you would put it across your shoulders, rejoicing,

Luk 15:6

and when you got home call in your friends and neighbors, saying, 'Celebrate with me! I've found my lost sheep!'

Luk 15:7

Count on it--there's more joy in heaven over one sinner's rescued life than over ninety-nine good people in no need of rescue.

Luk 15:8

"Or imagine a woman who has ten coins and loses one. Won't she light a lamp and scour the house, looking in every nook and cranny until she finds it?

Luk 15:9

And when she finds it you can be sure she'll call her friends and neighbors: 'Celebrate with me! I found my lost coin!'

Luk 15:10

Count on it--that's the kind of party God's angels throw every time one lost soul turns to God."

(we all know a lost sheep, would you leave your friends right now to go to them)

you may not have tomorrow

Tomorrow I have class in Sunday school and this is our lesson, but even though I was planning it for my kids, adults really need to take time and think of this too.

This week as I prayed before work, it was if there be someone that comes to the house for tour, allow there heart to be open to be able to minister in some way to them.

This week has been so full of stories, people in a ministry some place and the conversations have been so amazing, I give my tour and they stay sharing for at least 30 more minutes.

when I was younger I was so afraid to speak out for Jesus so I had a big cross I wore to school and if anyone asked about why I wore it I would share, thus the name Jesus freak followed me. yes was a freak for Jesus,and in the years to follow I have had times of growth and other times when I wasn't following His will in my life. I wasn't perfect in any way and I still grow daily with His love and word leading my life now.

But the years have gone by, I have seen so many of my friends die, ...unsaved.. my heart breaks for them, yes they were great people, they did a lot of great things for people.. but they never knew Jesus as there savior, they never gave their life to Him.

Being a good ...even great person does NOT get you through the gates of heaven, only believing in Jesus as the son of God and knowing in your heart He has died for your sins, will get you to heaven..plain and simple. its written no one goes to the father in Heaven but though the Son.

How many great, loving, amazing, giving people do you know..now do you know if they are saved, would you be willing to just ask them, and if they say they don't know Him could you lead them in the sinners prayer...

with things going on in the world right now, we can see for ourselves the time is getting close, yes we can pray for things to get better,but if we get down to the truth, some of these things are taking place because it was written in

Revelation and in other books to what was going to happen in the end times and when these things started happening to watch the signs from Heaven and know that time is getting near...

the time is getting close enough that if you know someone that isn't saved you need to go to them now before its to late for them, so many people die everyday and we never know when it will be our turn, when it will be there turn. if you know anyone that doesn't know Jesus, no matter what the age they may be, if there old enough to talk to, and old enough and still understand its not to late or to early. the time is never wrong to share Gods love with someone, that is why right now I am sharing this with you, I care and love each one of you and God does too. with all His heart.

the sinners prayer is so very easy

Jesus I know my life up to now hasn't been what would be pleasing to you, please forgive me for the things I have done in my past and as I give my life to you now, I trust in you and believe you are the Son of God and died on the cross for my salvation and my healing s of my body. I give my life to you now as a new creation, wanting to serve you and become what I was created to be, my life is now yours, guide me and as I study your word lead me in your ways, I love you and my life is now yours.

if you prayed this prayer, find another believer you can share with and talk to about the change you have made, let other Christians know so they can pray for you and keep you lifted up in there personal prayers,

My prayers are for all those that have read this that you will be touched. love to all of you.

WHY PRAYER WORKS

Scriptures 2 Ch 7;14/ Matt 5:44 / Matt 6:6 / Matt 21:13 / many more I will use as we go.

Over the last few months I have seen so very many prayers answered, some on Christian's, some non Christians, some small prayers and some very strong prayers where death could have been the result. Why are our prayers answered, how does it work, why does it seem some go unanswered, how does prayer feel to God,

In the bible we are told how to pray by Jesus Himself in Matt Mat 6:5 "And when you come before God, don't turn that into a theatrical production either. All these people making a regular show out of their prayers, hoping for stardom!

Do you think God sits in a box seat? Mat 6:6 "Here's what I want you to do: Find a quiet, secluded place so you won't be tempted to role-play before God. Just be there as simply and honestly as you can manage.

The focus will shift from you to God, and you will begin to sense his grace. Mat 6:7 "The world is full of so-called prayer warriors who are prayer-ignorant. They're full of formulas and programs and advice, peddling techniques for getting what you want from God. Mat 6:8 don't fall for that nonsense.

This is your Father you are dealing with, and he knows better than you what you need. Mat 6:9 With a God like this loving you, you can pray very simply. Like this: Our Father in heaven, Reveal who you are. Mat 6:10 Set the world right; Do what's best-- as above, so below. Mat 6:11 keep us alive with three square meals. Mat 6:12 Keep us forgiven with you and forgiving others. Mat 6:13 Keep us safe from ourselves and the Devil.

You're in charge! You can do anything you want! You're ablaze in beauty! Yes. Yes. Yes. Mat 6:14 "In prayer there is a connection between what God does and what you do. You can't get forgiveness from God, for instance, *without also forgiving others.*

Mat 6:15 If you refuse to do your part, you cut yourself off from God's part. God wants real not fake, He wants you to pray from your heart, not for who else may hear and say. man they are a strong prayer person,

God doesn't care about what they say, He cares about what is in your heart. Mat 5:14 "Here's another way to put it: You're here to be light, bringing out the God-colors in the world. God is not a secret to be kept. We're going public with this, as public as a city on a hill. Mat 5:15 If I make you light-bearers, you don't think I'm going to hide you under a bucket, do you?

I'm putting you on a light stand. Mat 5:16 Now that I've put you there on a hilltop, on a light stand--shine! Keep open house; be generous with your lives. By opening up to others, you'll prompt people to open up with God, this generous Father in heaven.

I think the song this little light of mine is perfect for this, you don't have to pray great prayers to help people, and lead them to Jesus, you let the glow of Jesus shine out of you, remember when you were pregnant or you may know someone that was or is. they have a new glow to them, they have life growing inside of them, they show it in there face, there actions and you can see this as the child grows.

ok now let's look at being a Christian, you should have a glow, a glow from Christ that is now living inside of you, people should be able to see this glow and the more you read your word, learning to pray and see things start happening in your life, this glow will grow too. the more you allow God control of your life the more he can use you.

In 2001 I was studying to become a Reiki Master, I thought that was a way to be able to help people and be able to have stronger connections to God....what I learned was so important to who I am now. they taught how to open your mind and spirit from the top of your head to the bottom of your feet, to allow the spirit of God to flow through your body out your hands, the hands would get so hot with the energy flowing through you that sometimes it would cause blisters on the hands.

They called on higher spirit. I called on God to flow through my hands, I see people that never knew any of this, and when they touch and pray over people there hands get hot, sometimes like a fire in their fingertips.

God is flowing through them so very strong. how because of their prayers, there prayers open the spirit to be used as a healing vessel. 2Ch 7:14 and my people, my God-defined people, respond by humbling themselves, praying, seeking my presence, and turning their backs on their wicked lives, I'll be there ready for you: I'll listen from heaven, forgive their sins, and restore their land to health. 2Ch 7:15 From now on I'm alert day and night to the prayers offered at this place.

We have to turn away from our past lives before becoming a Christian and become new creatures in and out of our spirit. so why do we have to ask for things so much. so many prayers for the same things, maybe God is seeing our hearts, we are to pray without ceasing 1 Thes 5:17 sometimes it seems prayer releases cumulative amounts of Gods power until with more prayers being said and getting stronger enough power is released to accomplish His will in that situation.

When we pray and we see the prayer isn't answered yet, the next time we pray harder, with more love, more strength, and more power in our words. when we get to the point of praying with passion Gods will can flow and we see answers, Isa 56:4 For GOD says: "To the mutilated who keep my Sabbaths and choose what delights me and keep a firm grip on my covenant, Isa 56:5 I'll provide them an honored place in my family and within my city, even more honored than that of sons and daughters. I'll confer permanent honors on them that will never be revoked. Isa 56:6 "And as for the outsiders who now follow me, working for me, loving my name, and wanting to be my servants-- All who keep Sabbath and don't defile it, holding fast to my covenant-- Isa 56:7 I'll bring them to my holy mountain and give them joy in my house of prayer. They'll be welcome to worship the same as the 'insiders,' to bring burnt offerings and sacrifices to my altar.

Oh yes, my house of worship will be known as a house of prayer for all people." Isa 56:8 The Decree of the Master, GOD himself, who gathers in the exiles of Israel: "I will gather others also, gather them in with those already gathered."

We are being prepared for that day when we will be in Gods house of prayer, we will learn while here on earth, how to pray, serve, worship, and adore with EVERYTHING in us, to pray and worship with passion, for the spirit of the living God to flow out of us. God has prepared a place for us Matt 25 : 34 at 25:34 "Then the King will say to those on his right, 'Enter, you who are blessed by my Father!

Take what's coming to you in this kingdom. It's been ready for you since the world's foundation. Mat 25:35 And here's why: I was hungry and you fed me, I was thirsty and you gave me a drink, I was homeless and you gave me a room, Mat 25:36 I was shivering and you gave me clothes, I was sick and you stopped to visit,

I was in prison and you came to me.' Mat 25:37 "Then those 'sheep' are going to say, 'Master, what you are talking about? When did we ever see you hungry and feed you, thirsty and give you a drink? Mat 25:38 And when did we ever see you sick or in prison and come to you?' When Christ lives in your heart, you have the heart of Christ in you, you treat others with more love, more understanding, more compassion, and you speak with your Father in heaven with passion, then you will see mountains move,

As I was speaking before, in the past few years I have seen so many things happen and healed that Drs couldn't explain, why. Because of prayer,because we asked and we shall receive. oh 16:24 Ask in my name, according to my will, and he'll most certainly give it to you. Your joy will be a river overflowing its banks! When you pray, ask knowing and believing, how do you really pray, do you pray for a few days and if nothing happen you slack off, or when you don't see answers pray harder, knowing the word is true and claim it with all that's in you. There is power in the spoken word, real power,

you can speak good or claim a curse. This is going to be ongoing study, this is a time God has really been pouring into my heart, leading me to power of prayers, power in claiming his word. you know this isn't the first time in history there were a lot of people that just refused to see the truth, some were doubters even when standing right beside Jesus.

There will always be those that don't believe, but for us that do, we stand strong on God's word and WE will be the ones to see healing s, family saved,

WE will see blessings not curses. Something to think about; you aren't born a prayer warrior; you are shaped and refined on a practice field of life, so get out on that field. and learn to be the strongest you can be, then you will say to that mountain of cancer be thou removed and it will flee, that mountain of poverty, the mountain of abuse, the mountain of sickness, the mountain of unemployment, be thou removed in Jesus name and it SHALL be moved.

BACK TO THE BASICS

You look around the world right now and so many people are asking why is this happening, what is going on with the world,why are people getting so many things wrong with them that never happened before.

well lets look for the answers from a very reliable book, the Bible;our scriptures will be found in Gen.1:27 / 9:3-4 /25:34 / proverbs 16:Proverbs 25:3 / Duet 14 / EC :20 / Isaiah 55:9

If we look in some of the chapters in the Bible we see a very loving God, one of mercy and grace. but we also see a father that loves his children so very much and allows them so much freedom and room to grow. but we also see God is a Father that at times has to deal with a child or children that don't follow his rules. when you were a small child did your parents allow you to do things that would hurt you and not try to stop you or warn you what your actions may do.

All through the scriptures God has tried to tell us what we are and how to take care of this temple (our bodies) in a way we can be the very best we can be ..a vessel that He can use for his glory. In Isaiah 55:9 Gods way of thinking and knowing what is best is so beyond our way of thinking. he knows what we need and how much..He created us.

When you have created something, you know everything that went into it, when you build a car you know what will keep it running and what will cause it to stop running.

When God created us he knows what we need before we do and its there when we ask. when he sees things working against us he has to reach out to protect us. when you have a child that keeps getting in to trouble with the car, you take the keys away don't you.

When we get to the point all we are placing into our bodies are destroying it sometimes drastic steps are taken to get us back on the right track.

So what are we suppose to do, what are we suppose to eat. lets get back to the basic needs and our diet book we have been given. lets go to the very beginning, Gen 1:27-29

We are to care for the earth, take care of it, not pollute it the way we have been, how far does our loving God have to go to get us back to the basics, to grow our own food,raise our own meats. families take care and feed there own. when there is over the amount we need to feed our family, share what we have with those who's crops didn't do as well.

We are given fruits and vegetables that produce seed to always have more for the next year, we have chickens,fish and other things that are good for us.

In Gen 9:3-4 we are told that we have to cook it, not eat raw meats that the blood is still flowing, not sushi we have land and waters that no longer can be used for food and we have to start thinking about going back to the basics. (read Duet 14)

So what are our basic needs,your Faith first of all then food water,shelter, clothing, and transportation, if we grow our own foods we know what goes into it, if you raise your own meats you also know what is going into them.

you can go one step farther, when you eat right you will feel stronger, in that you can be your own transportation at times. I know its easy to hop in your car and go to the next block to church, but how much better would it feel to walk to church.

As far as your health, if you start to eat right so many of the medicines people take would go out of business. grow flax seed and use it in your breads and flour, high cholesterol wont be in your problem list, stop eating junk and your heart will be stronger. God tells you over and over what you need to be doing. why is it you have to wait till something happens to you before yo start looking for the right way to do it.

I am so looking forward to the warm weather to get out and start walking. there are so many things I have had to change in my life and what I eat..why ..because I waited till something went wrong before I looked for ways to correct the problem without a bunch of pills. you know what I found is I had the answer in front of me all the time. The bible. God is showing us in the world we are living in right now. you dint have to start living in fear, go back to the basics and life in health the way He had planned from the very beginning.

FISHERS OF MAN

Did you ever wonder why Jesus said I will make you fishers of man, why did he choose fishermen and not some other profession.. ok lets take a look at what the great things are about a fisherman.

Well, one thing they know how to wait things out, ..to relax and take things easy. not to rush things,if something doesn't happen that day, it doesn't mean its a failure,to have peace in your spirit.. you go back a try again.

In being a witness for Christ what is it about your personality that would be good in reaching others, to take things easy, not push the issue, to be relaxed and have peace in your spirit. if you don't win them to Christ that day, you don't just give up, you try again.

Mat 4:19

They say that patience is a virtue ..why do you think that is, I feel its because if you have patience you have peace, if you have peace you can deal with everything life hands you.

What does it mean to you to have peace. the word says I will give you a peace that will pass all understanding. the things it takes to be a great fisherman is so needed if you are trying to bring someone into the fellowship of Christ.

You cant push, you cant control if the nibble, play with the word or swallow it deep and get the hook and are caught in all the love., there are some that will just toy with the hook,...Jesus had a story for this also.

In the story of the sower and the seed. all of Jesus stories give the ideas of the different people we will run across in our mission to bring others into Gods fellowship.

There will be those that just play with the bait. they know the word just enough to use it, to twist it and and use it in ways to make there point but not in a good way.

Then there are those that just nibble, they come to church, cry, and get you to open up to them and after they get what they need they dont come back any more. they come when they need something. just not the Lord.

Then there are the small fish, they know how to get the worm but not get hooked, they come to church, they want to learn, they want that peace so much but they just cant give up there safe little pond. where they know where everything is. to go on a new path is just to much.

But what makes it all so worth being patient, is when the person that has been so scared to leave their safe little pond, takes that step out of the water and learns to walk on the land.

They have a new joy, a new peace, a feeling of now knowing there was so much more outside of the pond they had been in, and now they want there friends to see life outside of the pond.

You know sometimes you can see the scum on the top of the pond when your in it looking up, but when you are finally out and look back to where you came from, you can see the filth you were in so clearly.

Are you ready to leave your safe little pond and learn to walk on the land..if you are then you too can become fishers of men. next time you throw your line out, think of this little message. think of someone you want to pull out of the scummy pond, and go to them with both your feet planted on the shores of Jesus.

Jesus said to them, "Come with me. I'll make a new kind of fisherman out of you. I'll show you how to catch men and women instead of perch and bass."

THE DREADED RECLINER

    To anyone that has been raised with one of these in their family, it strikes a cord of fear when your new husband says he wants to get one, I can remember all to well when my dad got his, till then he and my mom sat on the sofa and watched TV.
    Then in the early 70's he got a recliner, in a very short time things changed so much and we could see it and watch things happening, from the steps going upstairs we would watch and listen, to a young child this is what we could see.
    Before they would sit on the sofa, dad would have his arm around her, my sister and I would lay on the floor and we would all watch raw hide, Andy Griffith, I love Lucy ..I know this is really telling my age, but it was family time.
    Then the chair came into our home, at first it was cute, dad would sit back like he had a throne, mom would bring his coffee to him and we still watched TV, but over time little by little things started to change.
    Dad got some TV trays, meals were now shared in front of the TV, the talking we had at meal time was now gone, Deb would now sit on couch at one end me on the other, mom started doing her puzzles at the table.
    Then dad started falling asleep in the chair, he would come home from work, and go to his chair we would go upstairs because when he fell asleep the snoring was such we couldn't hear the TV any more, mom would fix dinner and we would go back upstairs, mom to the kitchen table to read her bible or do puzzles.
    Then she picked up needlepoint, she would now sit in the chair in the living room, doing that while dad watched TV, still not to much talking, and not hardly any sharing of the day and how it had been, the wall was going up.
    Since this was happening slowly, it wasn't hard to get used to it, but it all just stopped, the talking, cuddling, the closeness they once had was now gone, and now the lack of communication was causing stress in daily things that they used to be able to talk about.

Once a wall goes up, its as if the bond you had ,you now cant get past it anymore, what does a wall do and what are they used for, they are for separating, putting a divider between two rooms and that is what it does in a marriage also.

Sometimes a wall can be taken out and sometimes it cant, when the wall causes a false comfort zone, it is hard to remove, if any of you have a recliner and have had one for awhile you are relating to this very well aren't you. whether its yours or your husbands, you know what I am talking about.

For all you young people out there that are just starting out, before you go get your living-room set think about this, if you have to have a recliner, get the ones built in to a couch, where you can still sit close, hold hands, smile at each-other, talk to one another.

Don't let the dreaded chair cause a wall of separation in your family, when you marry it says the two become one, how can you stay one in spirit, mind and body when a wall comes up between you, we need to think why we were created for each other, wasn't it companionship, we were not meant to be alone, God saw this in His own creation of man Genesis 2 v 18.

When God created people, it was for pleasure of their company, when He created woman for the man it was for him to have company, she was his helpmate, what is a help mate, just look at the word help, ..to assist or aid, relief.

Now look at the word helpless.. without help, powerless, lacking strength, that's what we are without each other, when we start a new life with someone we have to be determined to keep that view of help mate in your mind set.

This isn't for the young ones only, even if you are going into a new relationship do to a death of a loved one or divorce, this does not change with age, we all need each other, we desire to have someone to share our lives with.

Don't let a chair cause a problem you may not be able to fix, stay close to that person you have chosen to spend your life with, then as the years go by they wont say..what happened to the way we used to be, always wanting to be close, sharing things...look around the room,is there a recliner in the room.

You know that could be the one invention that was created by the devil himself, JUST KIDDING, But how many people have been divided as a family because of this one thing, keep this in your mind and in your heart, the way things are getting in the world now days we really need a strong family unit, this one tiny thing may one way to keep a wall going up.

 I hope this may have helped someone, I know for me personally,when the time comes for my husband to get one of these things, ours will be a sofa one, our times on the couch are so very special and I wont allow one thing to stop this.

 We will be married 5 years the 9th of June 2012 and I pray we stay as close as we are now only grow closer as time goes by, but to do this we have to deal with each day one at a time, watch for the things that could harm our relationship and nip it in the bud.

when you look at the recliner in the store, is it going to be a chair or a wall ?

 I guess just think before you buy , it is your choice, make it wisely.

HOW TO AVOID THE PITY PARTY

How often in life do we go to parties? birthdays, weddings,anniversary,home comings, they are all fun times, good times, shared times.

These are all very good and we are always so happy when they get here and later through pictures after they are over.

But the party I am going to talk about today isn't a happy one, it isn't a enjoyed one and most of the time aren't thought of in a good way after they are over.

Its the pity party, we have all been to one, shared one and been invited to one, but I try very hard not to go there.

The word pity is a feeling of compassion or sorrow for another s misfortune, when some one hurts, you have the pain they are feeling inside of you too because of compassion.

This can be good, but it can also be the very thing that can bring you into there problems and this can be very bad.

You have people that know you have a tender heart, they tell you a sad story that just breaks your heart, you give them money to help put food on the table and pay bills.

Then you find out it went for things of pleasure and they didn't need it as bad as they had told you.

You have family that knows you very good, they can use your caring to get what they want and make you feel guilty if you don't give in.

Your spouses can use things to get their way, and when you don't give in, they get the you don't love me, you aren't the same any more, and use words to make their problem something only you can solve for them.

Then there is the big one, its name is (I) I just cant seem to do anything right,no one understands how I feel, no cares how I feel, no one seems to notice I am even around unless they want something.

We have all been invited to these pity party's haven't we, well it took a lot of going to them before I got to the point I can say, no thank you, you will have to go to that one alone.

I realized I cant do anything to make someone else happy, I cant do anything to make there bills go away,I cant do anything to make there problems go away.

(ps 103;13 2 Sam 12;6 john 4;11 Matt 18;33)
this is what the word says about pity, and find out why by reading the chapters.

To have joy..Neh 8;10 Is 55;12 and most important john 15;11 you cant place joy in anyone, only Jesus can place the joy in you, he gives peace beyond our understanding,in the word God gives direction for all the situations in your life that can take your joy away from you.

When you get saved, you are so filled with joy and all the angels in heaven rejoice with you.

But the devil has just lost one he had plans for, and he is ticked off big time, so he will try to attack you any way he can to steal your joy from you.

He will use friends to tell you things to bring you down, he will use family to make you feel sad and in despair, he will try to steal your wealth, health and happiness so you will forget the joy that had been in your heart.

In 3rd john 4 .. oh well that one is really short, just please read the whole thing, I mean it is really short.
When you are invited to a pity party, just see it for what it really is, it is the devil trying to steal your joy again.

He wants to bring you down with their problems, their worries, their insecurities, their past problems that they are still dealing with.

But if you allow God to speak to them and just explain, I cant come to the party, but I will pray for you, and with all your heart pray for them.

Pray for God to place joy in their heart, to meet their needs, to heal their pain, their body's, what ever the problem is they are having.

You have to realize, you aren't the great healer, God is, He alone can take the problems from them and heal there minds, heart,spirits, and fill their soul with his spirit.

There will always be pity parties, but you don't have to go any more, you have the right to say no more, and know in your heart, your prayers are in the long run going to help them more than you ever could have.

I will keep you all in my prayers, because I know this a really hard one to fight, its a daily battle for me, but I know I can do it and you can too'
Love and prayers to all who read this

IN MOUNTAIN AND VALLEY I PROTECT YOU

Wanting me to know and feel in my heart He is always with me,God has used these things this week showing me how the prayers of people are heard and they are answered, I went to a little store here in town, I saw this pendent and picked it up, it wasn't in English so I put it down, but there was something about it, picked it back up and after doing this a few times got it and took it home,then looked it up online. the story of the pendent

History on Pendent found 11/3/2010

The town's residents vowed that if God spared them from the effects of the bubonic plague ravaging the region, they would produce a play every ten years thereafter for all time depicting the life and death of Jesus. The death rate among adults rose from one in October 1632 to twenty in the month of March 1633. The adult death rate slowly subsided to one in the month of July 1633. The villagers believed they were spared after they kept their part of the vow when the play was first performed in 1634. Performances took place in 2000, and the most recent season of 102 performances took place from Saturday, May 15 until Sunday, October 3, 2010.

It can be said that the evolution of the Passion Play was about the same as that of the Easter Play, originating in the ritual of the Latin Church, which prescribes, among other things, that the Gospel on Good Friday should be sung in parts divided among various persons

Oberammergau Passion Play 2010

About half the inhabitants of Oberammergau are expected to take part in the once-a-decade Passion Play in the year 2010.

This means that over 2,000 villagers will bring the story of Jesus of Nazareth to life for the audiences that flock in from around the world. The play starts with Jesus entering Jerusalem, continues with His Death on the Cross and finishes with the Resurrection. As ever, this is an extraordinary community enterprise.

The pendent reads "In mountain and valley I protect you"

I have myself had a mass on my ovary removed by prayer in 2 days time, had 3 lumps removed from my right breast by prayer, I have seen cancer removed in a matter of a week end, there are so many things, I had a friend who had lump the size of walnut asked me to stand in for her and have my pastor pray for her, when we got home from church we got call the lump was gone.

Almost all these things were seen in ultra sounds or x rays, Dr appointment made to remove them in surgery, when prayed for and BELIEVING that prayers are heard and prayers are answered, things happen.

FOR FAITH

2Co 5:6 Therefore we are always confident and know that as long as we are at home in the body we are away from the Lord.

2Co 5:7 We live by faith, not by sight.

Jas 1:3 because you know that the testing of your faith produces perseverance.

Mat 17:20 He replied, "Because you have so little faith. Truly I tell you, if you have faith as small as a mustard seed, you can say to this mountain, 'Move from here to there,' and it will move. Nothing will be impossible for you."

Mat 9:2 Some men brought to him a paralyzed man, lying on a mat. When Jesus saw their faith, he said to the man, "Take heart, son; your sins are forgiven."

Mat 9:22 Jesus turned and saw her. "Take heart, daughter," he said, "your faith has healed you." And the woman was healed from that moment.

Luk 7:50 Jesus said to the woman, "Your faith has saved you; go in peace
Luk 17:5 The apostles said to the Lord, "Increase our faith!"

Luk 17:6 He replied, "If you have faith as small as a mustard seed, you can say to this mulberry tree, 'Be uprooted and planted in the sea,' and it will obey you.

Luk 22:32 But I have prayed for you, Simon, that your faith may not fail.

And when you have turned back, strengthen your brothers."

Rom 10:17 Consequently, faith comes from hearing the message, and the message is heard through the word about Christ.

Rom 14:23 But those who have doubts are condemned if they eat, because their eating is not from faith; and everything that does not come from faith is sin.

2Co 5:7 We live by faith, not by sight.

Gal 6:10 Therefore, as we have opportunity, let us do good to all people, especially to those who belong to the family of believers.

Jas 1:2 Consider it pure joy, my brothers and sisters, whenever you face trials of many kinds,

Jas 1:3 because you know that the testing of your faith produces perseverance.

Jas 1:4 Let perseverance finish its work so that you may be mature and complete, not lacking anything.

(FOR BEING DECEIVED)

Mat 24:10 At that time many will turn away from the faith and will betray and hate each other,

Mat 24:4 Jesus answered: "Watch out that no one deceives you.

Gal 6:9 Let us not become weary in doing good, for at the proper time we will reap a harvest if we do not give up.

Jas 1:22 Do not merely listen to the word, and so deceive yourselves. Do what it says.

1Co 6:9 Or do you not know that wrongdoers will not inherit the kingdom of God? Do not be deceived: Neither the sexually immoral nor idolaters nor adulterers nor male prostitutes nor practicing homosexuals

Luk 21:8 He replied: "Watch out that you are not deceived. For many will come in my name, claiming, 'I am he,' and, 'The time is near.' Do not follow them.

Rom 12:9 Love must be sincere. Hate what is evil; cling to what is good.

Rom 16:18 For such people are not serving our Lord Christ, but their own appetites. By smooth talk and flattery they deceive the minds of naive people.

(FOR DOUBT)

Mar 11:23 "Truly I tell you, if you say to this mountain, 'Go, throw yourself into the sea,' and do not doubt in your heart but believe that what you say will happen, it will be done for you.

Mat 28:17 When they saw him, they worshiped him; but some doubted.

Mat 28:18 Then Jesus came to them and said, "All authority in heaven and on earth has been given to me.

Mat 28:19 Therefore go and make disciples of all nations, baptizing them in the name of the Father and of the Son and of the Holy Spirit,

Mat 28:20 and teaching them to obey everything I have commanded you. And surely I am with you always,

Luk 24:38 He said to them, "Why are you troubled, and why do doubts rise in your minds?

Luk 24:39 Look at my hands and my feet. It is I myself! Touch me and see; a ghost does not have flesh and bones, as you see I have."

ANY TIME WE GO THROUGH DOUBT, ON OUR PRAYERS BEING HEARD, ON OUR HEALINGS, ON OUR GIFTS GOD HAS GIVEN, ON OUR FAITH, ON OUR VISIONS AND WHERE WE ARE BEING CALLED. WE HAVE TO SEE WHERE IT COMES FROM, ...HOW DO YOU KNOW IF DOUBT IS COMING FROM GOD TO CHANGE YOUR PATH..

IS GOD GOING TO BE GLORIFIED IN (CHANGING) YOUR THOUGHTS, IS HIS WILL GOING TO TAKE PLACE AND ARE YOU GOING TO SERVE OR SIT BACK AND WAIT FOR ANOTHER DOOR. ..

IF IT ISNT GOING TO GLORIFY ,... SERVE, ...BRING OTHERS TO KNOW AND TRUST HIM, ...TO SHARE HIS LOVE AND FORGIVENESS .. IF IT ISNT GOING TO DO ANY OF THESE, THEN NO

IT MAY NOT BE GODS WILL, BUT IF YOUR DIRECTION IS GOING TO DO ALL THE ABOVE I FEEL YOU MAY PRETTY MUCH BANK ON IT GOD IS LEADING YOU, PRAY HARD, FAST AND PRAY SOME MORE, SEEK GUIDENCE FROM YOUR PRAYER WARRIORS AND MOST OF ALL YOUR PASTOR.

DON'T LET THE DEVIL WIN YOU OVER THROUGH DEPRESSION

Scriptures; (Rev 12:11 NKJ)(1 Peter 2:24 KJV) (Rev. 12:10 NKJ)(Col 2:15 NKJ)

(James 4:7 NKJ) (1 Pet 5:10 NKJ) (Deut 30:19 NKJ)love this one)claim this one (Luke 10:19 NKJ)

When searching for a way to get point across I search the scriptures and other things where I need guidance

this time I was lead to a topic by (Steve Sampson a pastor and author,) this is one of the topics he had with some of mine added to bring about the point I was lead to speak about.. credit where credit is due" thank you for allowing God to pour through you.

Discouraged people exert no demand on the presence of God.

I think we all go through this at one time or another, feeling like the devil is winning..it's a lie and we have to see this!!

And they overcame him by the blood of the Lamb and by the word of their testimony, and they did not love their

lives to the death. (Rev 12:11 NKJ)

The blood of Jesus is all covering. All physical health, all mental health, all emotional health has been

purchased by the blood of Jesus. His precious blood not only paid for our sins, but for every possible sickness as

well. In fact, Jesus paid for our sicknesses with His blood before He paid for our sins.

"…by His stripes you were healed." (1 Peter 2:24 KJV)

He paid not only for our sins, but for our mental health. His blood covers the oppression that comes against our minds. His blood covers those distorted emotions because of things we've gone through. We don't have to buy

unbelief, we don't have to buy the lies of depression, we don't have to succumb to anything, because the blood of

Jesus has paid it all.

(1) WHAT ARE SOME THINGS THAT CAN HAPPEN IF WE DON'T CLAIM THIS DAILY_____

The devil is a liar. We have to see the most effective weapon he uses against the saints is discouragement. There is nothing more destroying than those stifling feelings of heaviness that border on hopelessness. But the good news

is that we have already been given authority over him. The accuser of our brethren…has been cast down. (Rev. 12:10 NKJ)

Stop Trying To Defeat The Devil

You cannot defeat the devil! He has already been defeated. we have to remember this at all times, His time has already come. He has been stripped of his power and authority. He only has the "power" to lie and oppress. (We have the authority through the blood of Jesus to resist his lies,) and to not buy the defeat he tries to sell us.

Having disarmed principalities and powers, He made a public spectacle of them, triumphing over them in it.

Col 2:15 NKJ)

A mistake commonly made by many Christians is that they are still trying to fight an enemy that has already been defeated." Nowhere "does the Scripture tell us to defeat the devil, but rather to resist him, and to exercise the

authority that we have already been given over him.

Therefore submit to God. Resist the devil and he will flee from you. (James 4:7 NKJ)

Gaining Strength By Resisting;But may the God of all grace, who called us to His eternal glory by Christ Jesus, after you have suffered a while, perfect, establish, strengthen, and settle you. (1 Pet 5:10 NKJ)

WHY IS IT SO HARD TO CLAIM THIS AT TIMES_____

It isn't always God's way to rescue us from some type of persecution or suffering. Sometimes He wants us to simply walk through it. As a result, He will perfect us, establish us, strengthen us, and settle us. sometimes we see this as God isn't answering our prayers, or worse he isn't listening to us, we have to see God works at His own pace, not ours.

(3) CAN YOU SHARE SOME THINGS YOU HAVE WALKED THROUGH THAT HAVE MADE YOU STRONGER._____

Frankly, resisting the devil is what makes us steadfast in the faith. this is what makes us strong in OUR faith.

God has a far greater purpose for us as individuals than we realize. He desires to make us strong in spirit. Strong, powerful, able to stand up to Satan and speak with power.

Christians have gained strength by resisting the lies of the devil and by exercising their faith in God.

It is good to remind yourself when you are feeling satanic opposition and oppression, that you are worth being resisted! God has His hand on you! when we are being attacked, it isn't the person the words are coming out of, its the spirit behind the words that has control of them.

Begin To Speak The Language Of Faith Many don't see victory because they refuse to embrace the language of faith. Speaking the language of faith is

simply agreeing with God's vocabulary, and not the devil's.

It isn't enough to know the promises of God and the goodness of God. We must come to a place of choice. We can either stay in the rut we are in, or we can say "Enough is enough" and begin to speak what God says.

To be discouraged, God says, "Choose life". Begin to agree with God. Rather than declare your circumstances and what your emotions dictate, begin to declare the greatness of God! always remember the power of the spoken word, it can bless or curse you.

It takes no faith (or character) to agree with your emotions. Emotions change by the minute. Anyone can declare the negative. Anyone can complain. Anyone can let his mouth spew out what his emotions feel at that given

moment. Many spend their entire lives letting their vocal chords record what their emotions feel.

HOW MANY TIMES DO WE SPEAK BAD THINGS OVER OURSELVES_
_____ But God has given you and me a choice.

I call heaven and earth as witnesses today against you, that I have set before you life and death, blessing and cursing; therefore choose life, that both you and your descendants may live; (Deut 30:19 NKJ)

God will wait for you to get tired of the old habitual rut you are in. He will politely wait, and not stop you from wasting years. You can let it be your choice to continue plodding down the road of discouragement and

depression, and defeat. Or – you can rise up in faith and begin to speak His language. Without faith, it is impossible to please God. This is your choice.

The language of faith agrees with God. Faith declares God's faithfulness, and declares everything else a lie. You must not be concerned about what natural circumstances dictate, because from now on, God is your source. If

things get worse at first, it doesn't matter, because God is seated on the throne of your life. Because you have begun to align your speech with His Word (speaking the language of faith), there will inevitably be results.

It is of necessity to repent. Repentance is not shedding a bucket of tears, but it simply means – about face!

You must make a quality decision such as, "I repent of agreeing with the devil's lies, I am choosing to agree with God, and speak His language."

Whoever offers praise glorifies Me; and to him who orders his conduct aright

I will show the salvation of God."

(Ps 50:23 NKJ)

Fear is abnormal. God didn't create us to live in fear. Worry is abnormal. God didn't create us to live with worry.

Joy is normal! Peace is normal! The gospel is good news which dictates our standard of living. Refuse to embrace fear and worry and discouragement. Embrace the promises of God! It is your choice. CLAIM THIS IN JESUS NAME. CLAIM IT.

God has given you and me authority over all the power of the enemy.

Behold, I give you the authority to trample on serpents and scorpions, and over all the power of the enemy, and

nothing shall by any means hurt you. (Luke 10:19 NKJ)

WHAT ARE SOME AREAS WE NEED TO CLAIM THIS IN_____

Nothing Makes You Grow Faster Than Seeking The Lord, Nothing Makes You Grow Faster Than Seeking The Lord

Human nature, including Christian human nature, gravitates to seeking the advice or opinion of people, rather than God. We find it easier to relate to someone we can see, rather than He Whom we cannot see.

Of course it is not wrong to seek out counsel and encouragement from other people, but true change and growth comes when we seek the Lord.

Making an investment of time in uninterrupted prayer creates an unexplainable strength to the human spirit.

Finding another person to "unload" the problem on will bring a temporary support and relief.

When the enemy of your soul resists you, it usually means one of two things. Either you are on the verge of a breakthrough, or you are on the right track with God and the devil is trying to discourage your efforts.

Rather than embracing discouragement, we can rejoice that the devil is worried about us.

No wonder James tells us to rejoice when we are going through trials!

My brethren, count it all joy when you fall into various trials, knowing that the testing of your faith produces patience. (James 1:2-3 NKJ)

God is allowing trials to being forth a permanent result of character in your inner man.

God desires to promote us. He wants to take us to higher and higher levels and dimensions in Him. But no promotion takes place without an exam.

Blessed is the man who endures temptation; for when he has been approved, he will receive the crown of life which the Lord has promised to those who love Him. (James 1:12 NKJ)

Promotion is on the way! Be encouraged!

WHEN CHRISTIANS HAVE DOUBTS.

Scriptures are; 2 Cor 5;6-7 / James 1;3 / For faith-Matt 17:20 -9;2 -9;22 / Luke 7:50 / 17;5 / 22;32

Rom 10;17-/ 14;23 / 2 cor 5;7 / Gal 6;10 / James 1;2-4

for being deceived-Matt 24;10 / 24;4 / Gal 6;9 / Rev 12;9/ James 1;22 / 1cor 6-9 / Luke 21;8 / Rom16;18

for doubt-Matt 14:28-31 (Mark 11;23 what you can do with faith) Matt 28;17 Luke 24;38

    Yes, it happens to all of us at one time or another,we have a faith that could move mountains, then something happens we don't understand and its changed to , where is this God I have put my faith in.

    We first have to know one thing, as soon as you trust and believe in Jesus, the devil gets supper ticked off, he had painful things for you to do to people, he had people picked out for you to destroy and cause problems to.

    Now your going to be working for the other team, that made him angry, so now he has to try to get you back. He will deceive you any way he can and try to make it look like God did it,he will put doubts in your head, cause you to go through things that hurt your emotions and spirit.

    To the point you start thinking, ok where is this God that is suppose to be so great, all I have gone through since I gave my heart to him is bad, I don't know if this is worth it or not.

HAVE ANY OF YOU GONE THROUGH SOMETHING AND THOUGHT THIS, WONDERED WHERE GOD WAS_____

    Oh please.. don't let the devil deceive you that way, you have to know its him doing that not God, the devil wants you back. But remember, just as heaven is real, so is hell, please keep this in mind, its all very real, the torment, fire, endless pain and suffering. please it is so real.

In 2 Cor 5;6-7 faith is believing even if you cant see it,sometimes I think people in Missouri have a harder time with this,its the show me state and a lot of people I know have a feeling of wouldn't Jesus show up if it would make someones faith stronger.

But if He showed up at places all the time, how long would it be before you would just think it was normal, faith is believing without seeing.

     He gave his life for you to have a way to go to the father in heaven,he hung on that cross for you and me,if he had to show himself for you to believe,its like doing something so special for someone and they don't even say thank you.

Eph 6;10 take up the shield, protect yourself from being deceived with it, prayer can shield you if you ask for it. You have to trust that the word of God is true,it will be attacked by those who work from the leadership of the devil.

They will try to put thoughts in your head to make you doubt,wonder,and in time if you aren't very careful change your way of thinking back to where it was before.

DO YOU HAVE FRIENDS OR FAMILY THAT TRY TO PLACE DOUBTS IN YOUR MIND WITH OUT REALLY MEANING TO? WHAT ARE SOME WAYS WE CAN FIGHT THIS_____

If we don't fight this when we see it happening action will cause reaction....Then you will be filled with depression, anger, bitterness, and memories of your past that caused you pain, so you will be in torment again, right where the devil wants you.

In James 1;3 God try s so hard to warn you of things that will come you way,he knows how the mind of the devil works. But He also shows you how to beat it, as Christians..there will be trials, testings, and hardships, but they aren't from God, they are the devil trying to cast doubt in you ,you need to read your scriptures to find what you need to fight it, I know this is a lot but I am going to give you some scriptures to help you.

Get a pen and paper and in your own time, look these up and really read them, its all in the word if you look, don't go on the internet looking for your answers,there are to many people out there that aren't speaking for your soul to be with God but on the contrary, working to lead you off the right path.

You don't need the internet if you search the bible, its all in there, warnings,and how to fight it. ok here's the list.

For faith-Matt 17:20 -9:2 -9:22 Luke 7:50 -17:5-22:32

Rom 10:17-14:23 2 cor 5:7 Gal 6:10 James 1:2-4

for being deceived-Matt 24:10 24:4 Gal 6:9 Rev 12:9 James 1:22 1cor 6-9 luke 21:8 rom16:18

for doubt-Matt 14:28-31 (Mark 11:23 what you can do with faith) matt 28:17 Luke 24:38 there was still some doubt,even when they saw

     Faith can be strong or weak, strong when things are going your way and weak when things go wrong, when its weak you don't see the way God is working for you, you are blinded by your doubt.

     The thing love is blind, well so is doubt,when your in love, you only see the good in that person,people can warn you of things but you don't see it, your blinded because of you love. The same is true with doubt, it blinds you to the truth, others can tell you things God is doing for you, in you through you and can do for you.

     But the doubt will keep you from believing it, you miss your healing, your blessing, you miss the doors God was trying to open for your future to be a blessing for you. You miss the future of doing what you dreamed of because your doubt shut the door, you went off the path that He had prepared for you with one blessing after another if you kept your faith in him strong so he could guide you.

     Don't go back to your doubting mind, your doubting way of thinking, you miss out on so much, I have something going on in my life right now that could be a real worry if I didn't know for a fact God was going to use it some how.

     I have part time job that pays 6.65 a hour, I still have bills, responsibilities, but I also know God is in control, we will have our needs met and in some way God will get the blessing and praise for this. He is bringing people in my path everyday that I can speak with, I leave my book on the table in the back to read and they can ask questions that open a door to share with them.

God is opening so many doors and allowing me to have more vision of the future with Tom in a whole new area of ministry, we are both so very excited and this will need so very much prayer, we have to search for Gods will each step of the way, it may be in a few years or it could happen sooner, but it will be Gods time not ours.

Because of the things we have gone through in our lives we are going to reach out to others that are going through them and show them love and understanding from someone that has been in their shoes, knows the pain, fear, hopelessness, and seeing no way out. BUT GOD.

We have prayed for confirmation. It was given, we are now praying for information, area, legal issues. We know God is in control and we are seeking His guidance in this every step we take, to not move to fast and to stay strong on His path, not listen to the negative remarks or have doubts on our faith, our abilities . But to allow God to have all of us and use us in new ways to reach out as a husband and wife team.

You have to keep your eyes on Him for him to show you what he wants to do in your life, don't doubt, pray.. don't be deceived, pray.. have faith in a God that loves you and wants to use you and help you, all you have to do is ask and you will see what I mean.'just give it a chance, don't let the devil win you back to his way of thinking, you will only have pain in your life if you do.

I will have all of you in prayer today, for your faith to be strong, and the spirits sent out to attack you be sent back to where they came from...that God will shield and protect you so your faith can get back to where it needs to be.

A CLOAK FOR YOUR SINS

Scriptures John 15:12 – 21

In John 15, Jesus tell us how we are to love, and why we should love in His name, in John 15:12 He says this is my commandment to you, that you love one another as I have loved you.

In this He says to all of us, to love one another to the point that we should give your life for that person, how many of you would do that for a friend, Jesus has called us friends, that in His own words someone you would lay your life down for, a true friend doesn't lie to each other, or keep things away from there knowledge that could help them.

(1) as much as you love your friend, do you honestly feel you would die for them_____

Jesus told us all things, he has kept nothing from us, in John 15:15 he says all the Father in heaven has made known to Him he has made known to us.

(2) What can we do in His name?_____ In verse 16 we read, He has chosen us and ordained us that we should go out to all the world, that anything we ask in His name will be given to us.

In verse 21 He says that we will go through trials for His name sake because of the people that know not the father, how can anyone who doesn't know Jesus understand about the love He has to give.

Before you heard of Jesus, you could hide your sins and make excuses for them, but after your salvation you have no cloak for your sins before man or from God, as Christians we need to be the sort of people that are set apart from the world, this takes time and prayer and a lot of study.

In verse 22 Jesus tells us, before you know the truth of Jesus Christ you had not sin, but after he spoke to them, they had no cloak for their sin, by His death on the cross and His resurrection and the spirit that came to live in us, we gave our cloak to Him, that now we will no longer hide behind the reasoning of (I didn't know).

You know so often we only think of the ten commandments in the old testament, and we don't think of the times Jesus says I command you or this commandment I give to you. We don't know because we haven't read the bible enough to really know what it says for us to do, that's why we find it so hard to lead the christian walk, we don't know what it is.

when you read the bible, do you read it or study it, what difference do you find when you really search the scriptures_____

There are so many things God wants to bless you with, but you will never know what they are if you don't pick up the bible and read them , you have to read to learn, when Jesus talks of love, it is so clear to see what He wants us to do, we are to love one another as He has loved us, we are to follow in His footsteps in all ways.

We are walk as He walked, talk as He talked, act as He would act and love the way He would have loved, but how are we to know Jesus and know how He would do things if we don't read about Him, you can hear people talk about him, listen to songs about Him, see plays, but to really know Him you have to read and pray, only then do you know the man He really was and is.

Only then can He become a part of you, only then can others see His love in you, by your actions, what would make you feel better? If someone came up to you and said, oh really.. I didn't know you were a christian, or if they said I always knew you were. I could tell by the way you act and how you speak.

Would they be surprised to see you at a church, or would they expect to see you there, the way we are outside the walls of the church is what God sees, and all the other people that are watching you, are you the same in the church as you are on the outside?

(4) when did you get to the point of really letting Jesus flow out of you where people could see it_____

Was Jesus just the son of God on Sundays or was he the same day after day, what if He only saved people on Sundays or had a day He was just to busy. He was the same yesterday, today and forever, He never changes, we are the ones that change and make Him ashamed of us.

Yes we shame Him, we don't have a cloak of invisibility with God, He sees through all the dirt, all the sin, all the lies, all the lust, cussing, yes we shame Him, when we know the right thing to do and we do the wrong thing anyway, its sin and its shame to him.

Are you still hiding behind your cloak? Do you really think God doesn't know what you have done, didn't see what you did, didn't hear the words that came out of your mouth, if you do you still have so much to learn.

If you have been living this way, are there things you have done, thought or said that you know weren't of God? right now, ask Him to forgive the sins you have been doing, the ones you have tried to hide from him, ask forgiveness and make a vow to try never to do them again, ask for the strength to stop doing the wrong things.

Put the cloak you have been hiding behind on the cross, give it to Jesus and let Him know that all things are His from now on, that nothing will be kept from Him any longer.

That you will be a vessel to be used for His glory, not any of my own but that all praise will go to Him and His holiness. In Jesus name I claim this promise, ask anything in my name and it will be.

My spirit will be made stronger, to keep me from the weakness that Satan can use in me, I bind Satan in all ways from doubting and fear, to have and claim the power of prayer and power in Jesus name. To know that our lives, our children, our relationships, all of it are in Gods hands, that nothing is hidden from Him,

Now lift your hands up to him, give Him your cloak and become His vessel.

CALLED FOR A PURPOSE

What does it mean to have purpose ? well lets see what the word means..a desired goal, an intention, the use for which something was made or had a intention for.

We have a lot of scriptures for this one so I hope you all have your bibles or at least a pen to write them down. because to find your purpose in life you have to know the whole reason your here.
Eph 1;11 / Eph 3;11 /Eccl 3;1 /Acts 2;23 / Rom 8;28 /9;17 /Gal 3;19 / 2 Cor 9;7

From the very beginning God had His reasons for creating you, in Eccl 3;1 He has a season for everything, birth,death, planting and harvest, you were not born at the wrong time. this is the very time you were suppose to be here.

God has always had a design for your life, a reason for you to be here, in Eph 1;11 He wants a glorious life for you, glorious living in the bibles own words, He has always had a plan for your life to be good for you and to be a blessing.

In Rom 8;28 for we know that all things work together for good to them that love God and those that are called for a purpose, ..in Rom 9;17 it is said He hand picked people for things He had plans for, He has also hand picked you.

We are all well thought out plans of God, Acts 2;23 even with His own sons death, every detail was in place, planned out. for us to have salvation through His only Son, it was planned for us, out of love.

Even when Jesus could have asked His Father in heaven to take this cup from Him, Jesus knew He had a purpose John 12;27 He knew this was why He was born and knew He had a path He was to follow.

1 John 3;8 Jesus was sent as Gods plan against sin, to abolish the devils ways, God wanted us to have a way to always come to Him no matter what sin was in our lives, we have the way before us to be forgiven. and it was all part of the great plan for your life. and mine.

Ok now you may ask, how do I find my purpose in life, I think this is a question we all have asked ourselves, and that right there is the problem.. we ask ourselves, as humans we haven't the understanding to find the answers to that question.

But in putting your faith in Christ and following His leadership we can find the answer, if you believe with all your heart that you do have a plan, you do have a purpose you will be lead to the right path that God has planned for you.

1. what do you feel you are blessed with?-_____

2. what do others see you are blessed with_____

3. what is your desire to do with this gift_____

We have to search daily and be open to Gods calling in our lives, when I got the calling to the ministry, I thought God had made a big mistake, I didn't have the nerve to go up and talk to people and preach to them.

I didn't have the vocabulary to talk like I knew what I was talking about, it was very hard for me to put in words what I was thinking and trying to say, I had three small children at home, driving a school bus everyday.

God you have to show me how I am to follow your will in this, I have no idea what to do, but show me and I am yours, I want to do what ever it is your leading me to do. the doors were opened to me for a teaching through the mail, I took it, and within a year I was able to be ordained.

Another door opened and a building became open free of charge for the bible studies, and the New Beginnings was formed, then the calling got stronger and the pull was to reach people world wide.

Ok God I cant leave home with three children and be a missionary any place, my thinking was this had to be wrong feeling on my part, I had to fight this feeling for years and tried to push it away.

Then in 2007 my son had me open a my space website to have more contact with him, I thought my profile page is going to be a testimony page, ..the response was amazing, the more I talked to people and there prayer request, questions, I knew with all that was in me this is what I was to do.

I would be able to reach the world for God just as He had called me to do, I now have 4 ways through the internet to get His word out to the world, I have found my purpose, it was to be a vessel for God to use.

I feel Him leading me in all I do with the studies, I am willing to do what ever I can to get His word out to the many people that are searching for answers, one thing I have found through all of this, I have to be willing to be still and listen, not just pray and go.

4. are you willing to step out in faith _____

5. what would the one thing to hold you back _____

  And don't do as I did and try to find reasoning in it, sometimes at first it may not make since to you, but its because all the pieces aren't in place yet.
  It may take time for all your doors to open, but don't give up, in time your doors will open and you will see it was all a part of plan that was made from the time of your birth, it will all fit together.
  For His plan to work in me it took many roads, some good that were His will, and some not good when I didn't listen and went my own way, it took Him 13 years to get my head on straight.
In 2 Cor 9;7 He wants us to take time and really think things over, prepare and make up your mind, its your choice, then you will serve with a joyful heart, God loves a giver that delights in giving.

6. How many times have you jumped in feet first with out talking it over with God first?--- _____

7. what was the out come _____

  We all have a purpose in life, Gods plan is a good one and you will be so very blessed, but you have to stay in His will to find this, your life cant be filled with all sorts of sin and Him use you for His Glory,
  We all have sins in our lives that need forgiven, we have to ask daily for this, but the heart that is pressing in and going forward in His word and His ways will be a useable vessel for Him to use.

8. what are some things that can keep you from being a useable vessel _____

9. what can we do to help each other to reach our purpose _____

  You know sometimes when we go through something really awful we wonder why God why did this have to happen to me, I thought that many times, but what I have found, with being raped and going through the healing from it and becoming a stronger woman through it, when that 16 year old came to me the night she was raped, I was able to help her get through that *night because I could share her pain, I had really been there at her age, you turn that pain to a blessing when you help someone with your victory.*

I know what it all feels like because I have been there, in so many things I can now reach out to someone going through that time in their life and show them they to can be a survivor. They can grow through this. Turn every pain to a victory and God wins.

(pray for each other is the most important, share things with each other so they know they aren't the only one feeling this, keep you mouth shut outside of these rooms, we don't share to gossip, we share to help and pray.)

My prayer for you today is that you find your calling, find the place that you feel you have purpose. God has a plan for each of us, all we have to do is allow Him to speak to us, and be open enough to listen.

My prayers are with all of you, may God open your eyes and your heart to what He has planned for you, and may He pour His blessings all over you, prayers and Big Hugs to the world, Susie

COMMUNICATION, WHATS IT REALLY MEANS

scriptures are; Amos 3;3 Leviticus 26 1-13   Heb 10:24-25 Rev 3:20 / Psalms 42:7 Zechariah 7:13 James 4:6-8 Proverbs 18:21/ 26:22/ 1 Peter 3:10

WHAT IS COMMUNICATION WELL, LETS SEE, THE DICTIONARY SAYS IT IS THE ACT OF TRANSMITTING IDEAS THROUGH WRITTING OR SPEACH, THE MEANS TO TRANSMIT MESSAGES BETWEEN PERSONS AND PLACES, WELL THATS THE FACT OF THE WORD. BUT WHAT DOES THE WORD MEAN IN RELATIONSHIPS?

YOU SEE SO VERY MANY TIMES TO PEOPLE, THE WORD MEANS HEAR ME WHEN I SPEAK, AND THEY WANT YOU TO HEAR WHAT THEY ARE SAYING. BUT THERE IS SO MUCH MORE TO THAT WORD, YES IT DOES MEAN GETTING A POINT ACROSS, A IDEA, A PLAN, BUT IF THE PERSON YOU ARE SPEAKING WITH DOESNT WANT TO HEAR WHAT YOU HAVE TO SAY, THE COMMUNICATION IS LOST.

FOR THERE TO REALLY BE COMMUNICATION, THERE HAS TO BE A PERSON ON THE OTHER END THAT WANTS TO LISTEN TO WHAT YOU ARE TRYING TO SAY , AND NOT JUST BE THINKING WHAT THEY ARE WANTING TO SAY BACK.

1.how often when you talk to someone can you tell they aren't listening, how can you tell?
_____
2.do you, in a argument have planned what you are going to say before you speak_____

IN ORDER TO REALLY UNDERSTAND WHAT COMMUNICATION MEANS WE HAVE TO LOOK AT ANOTHER WORD, COMMUNION , LETS SEE, THE DICTIONARY SAYS ITS THE MUTUAL SHARING OF FEELINGS AND THOUGHTS, A RELIGIOUS

FELLOWSHIP BETWEEN BELIEVERS AND THE CHURCH.

IN THE ART OF COMMUNICATING WE HAVE TO HAVE COMMUNION WITH EACHOTHER, WE HAVE TO HAVE FELLOWSHIP WITH EACHOTHER, WHAT IS FELLOWSHIP, A FRIENDLY RELATIONSHIP, A CONDITION OR FACT OF HAVEING COMMON INTERSEST, IDEAS, OR EXPERIENCES.

3. what does the bible call fellowship -Amos 3;3 Leviticus 26 1-13   Heb 10:24-25 Rev 3:20 _what is it to you_____

4.what is communion in the bible - Psalms 42:7 Zechariah 7:13 James 4:6-8 what does it mean to you_____

NOW THIS MAY SEEM LIKE WE ARE STUDING THE DICIONARY, BUT TO FULLY UNDERSTAND HOW WE ARE TO COMMUNICATE WITH ONE ANOTHER, WE HAVE TO FIRST UNDERSTAND THE WORD AND WHAT IT MEANS.

WE HAVE TO UNDERSTAND IF COMMUNICATION IS LOST ..BETWEEN CHILDREN, SPOUSES, STUDENTS, BOSSES, CHURCH MEMBERS, ANYONE, THE RELATIONSHIP IS SOMETIMES LOST TOO AND THAT IS WHY WE HAVE TO KNOW THE WORD AND WHAT IT REALLY MEANS.

WHEN WE LOOK BACK TO GENISIS, WHEN GOD CREATED MAN, THE ONE THING THAT HE SAW WAS IT WASNT GOOD FOR MAN TO BE LONELY, WOMAN WAS CREATED FOR COMPANIONSHIP, THE COMPANIONSHIP AND COMPLEATNESS THE GOD INTENDED FOR MARRIAGE GROW OUT OF COMMUNICATION, AS TWO PEOPLE SHARE EACH DAY AND THE MEANING OF THEIR LIVES.

WE HAVE TO SEE THAT COMMUNICATEING ISNT JUST TALKING, IT BEING WILLING TO LISTEN ITS BEEN ESTIMATED THAT USUALLY A PERSON ONLY HEARS ABOUT 20 % OF WHAT IS SAID, SO WHAT IS REALLY NEEDED IS A LISTENING SKILL. LISTENING EFFECTIVELY MEANS THAT WHEN A PERSON IS

TALKING , YOUR NOT THINKING ABOUT WHAT YOU WANT TO SAY WHEN THEY STOP, INSTEAD YOU ARE TOTALLY TUNED IN TO WHAT THEY ARE SAYING.

ITS REALLY CARING ABOUT WHAT THE OTHER PERSON IS SAYING, SO MANY TIMES WE DONT WANT TO LISTEN AS MUCH AS WE WANT TO BE HEARD. THE OLD SAYING STICKS AND STONES MAY BREAK MY BONES BUT WORDS WILL NEVER HURT ME IS VERY FALSE. WORDS CAN CUT SO DEEP SOMETIMES THEY NEVER HEAL.

5. have you been hurt by words, how long did it take to heal_____

6. have you hurt someone with words if so how is the relationship now_____

IN PROVERBS 18 :21 (Pro 18:21 The tongue has the power of life and death, and those who love it will eat its fruit.)
DEATH AND LIFE ARE IN THE POWER OF THE TONGUE, PROVERBS 26 :22 (Pro 26:22 The words of a gossip are like choice morsels; they go down to the inmost parts.)
A WHISPER GOES DOWN TO THE VERY INNERMOST PART OF THE BODY. YOU CAN GET A HUGE HORSE TO GO WHERE YOU WANT WITH A VERY SMALL BIT IN ITS MOUTH, A TINY RUDDER CAN GIVE CONTROL OVER BIG BOATS, A GREAT FORREST CAN BE BURNT DOWN WITH A TINY MATCH, ...AND SO MARRIAGES AND FRIENDSHIPS CAN BE DESTROYED WITH A TINY WORD.

WHAT WE SAY TO OUR HUSBANDS, WIVES, CHILDREN, FRIENDS CAN TURN THINGS AROUND JUST LIKE THE SMALL RUDDER AND WE END UP GOING IN CIRCLES,

WE HAVE TO THINK BEFORE WE SPEAK IN 1ST PETER 3;10 (1Pe 3:10 For, "Whoever among you would love life and see good days must keep your tongue from evil and your lips from deceitful speech.)
IF YOU WANT A HAPPY LIFE, KEEP CONTROL OF YOUR TONGUE AND GUARD YOUR LIPS.

FOR COMMUNICATION TO REALLY WORK WE HAVE TO HAVE A INTIMATE RELATIONSHIP THAT IS BUILT ON MUTUAL TRUST AND UNDERSTANDING, YOU HAVE TO REALLY GET TO KNOW THAT PERSON TO BE ABLE TO COMMUNICATE WITH THEM,

IN OUR RELATIONSHIP WITH OUR FATHER IN HEAVEN, WE ALSO NEED TO APPLY THESE THINGS, WE CAN GO TO HIM AND TALK AND TELL HIM OUR FEARS,OUR THOUGHTS,OUR THANKSGIVEINGS,AND ASK TO BE USED FOR HIS GLORY. WE CAN GO THROUGH ALL THE STEPS WE FEEL ARE THE RIGHT WAY TO DO IT, BUT IF WE DON T GO THE NEXT STEP IN COMMUICATEING, AND LISTEN WE ARENT GOING TO KNOW WHAT PATH HE HAS FOR US, WE WILL MISS IT.

WE HAVE TO TAKE THE TIME TO REALLY LISTEN, NOT JUST TALK, THEN WE WILL HAVE COMMUICATION, THEN WE WILL HAVE COMMUNION, THEN WE HAVE FELLOWSHIP, THEN WE HAVE A RELATIONSHIP THAT HAS A STRONG BOND.

WHEN WE KNOW WE ARE GOING TO HAVE A TALK WITH SOMEONE, AND ITS IMPORTANT, WE MUST PRAY FIRST, ASK GOD TO HELP YOU FIND THE RIGHT WORDS TO GET YOUR POINT ACROSS WITHOUT HURTING THEIR FEELINGS. ASK HE OPEN YOUR EARS TO BE A GOOD LISTENER SO YOU WILL UNDERSTAND THEIR THOUGHTS AND IDEAS, PRAY FOR THERE TO BE A PEACE IN THE SITUATION THAT A SOLLUTION CAN BE FOUND OR ANSWERS TO A SITUATION.

PRAY FOR HIS GUIDANCE AND THEN BE WILLING TO STAY PUT AND LISTEN TO HIM, DONT JUST PRAY PUT IT ALL IN GODS HANDS AND WALK AWAY, YOU HAVE TO BE WILLING TO LISTEN TO GOD IF YOU ARE GOING TO BE ABLE TO LISTEN IN A CONVERSATION.

GOD WANTS US TO HAVE FELLOWSHIP WITH HIM AND WITH EACHOTHER, IT IS HIS PLAN FOR US TO BE ABLE TO BE A HELPMATE FOR EACHOTHER, HE GIVES THE MANUAL WE NEED TO KNOW HOW TO FIX PROBLEMS, BUILD STRONG FRIENDSHIPS, MARRIAGES, RAISE STRONG CHILDREN, ITS ALL THERE. BUT WE HAVE TO BE WILLING TO PICK IT UP AND READ IT, THE BIBLE, ITS A LIGHT TO YOUR PATH.

WHY IS ALL OF THIS SO IMPORTANT YOU MAY WONDER, WELL HOW CAN YOU BE A WITNESS FOR CHRIST IF YOU DON'T KNOW HOW TO SPEAK WITH OTHERS, HOW CAN YOU REACH YOUR FAMILY MEMBERS,FRIENDS NEIGHBORS IF YOU DON'T

KNOW HOW TO LISTEN

SO GO GET YOUR BIBLE, BRUSH THE DUST OFF OF IT AND START READING, WE CANT JUST READ IT ONCE A WEEK TO GROW, IT HAS TO BE A DAILY WALK FOR YOU TO HAVE COMMUNION.

YOU WILL FIND THE ANSWERS YOU NEED, AND GUIDENCE HE WANTS TO GIVE YOU.

I HOPE I HAVE COMMUNICATED IN A GOOD WAY TODAY, NOW ITS UP TO YOU IF YOU LISTEN.THIS IS PART ONE OF TWO, MORE TO COME (NEXT WEEK), HAVE A VERY BLESSED DAY,GOD IS THERE WAITING TO TALK TO YOU..COMMUNICATE WITH HIM.

COMMUNICATION. Part 2

This is part two of communication, in part one we covered how to communicate with each other, how to have two way conversation, where not only do we get our point across, but we allow the other person to get their point across calmly.

In part two we are going to go a little deeper into this, but in the area of having conversation with our creator, our Father in heaven, how do we have conversation with our God, our Savior, our Father.

When we were small I know we all, or most of us learned to say our prayers at night, we folded our hands, bowed our heads and started our prayer, now I lay me down to sleep.

It was a very short simple little prayer, but it was the start of having a conversation with God, short simple, and the same night after night. but as we get older we learned to add things to this little prayer.

We added, please make mommy well, please take care of my sister, my pet that was lost, our booboos, so many tiny things, that God heard as we prayed, all our prayers He He hears, and feels our thoughts, happiness, sadness, He understands it all.

But now He wants a closer fellowship with us, He wants us to have communication with Him, We don't talk to our friends the same way we did as a child, our ways of expressing ourselves changed as we grew up.

We were closer now, shared things with each other more, cried with each other, laughed with each other, shared our good times and our bad times, and that is what God wants us to do with Him.

When is the best time to pray, well in Psalms 55:16-18 David says we are to pray in the morning, afternoon and evening /as we greet the day, see the light of the sun or the stars in the sky, a thankful prayer can flow from your lips.

In the afternoon, as you are busy with the things of the day, Just talking to God as a friend that is by your side, tell Him whats in your heart, if your getting angry at coworker, children, spouse, or even yourself. let God know what your feeling and ask Him to help you with those feelings.

In the evenings, when its starting to quiet down around the house, kids are in bed, dishes are done, just a time to relax, it is the perfect time to talk to God, ask Him to forgive the times during the day when your actions, thoughts, or words weren't something that would bring glory to His name.

Talk to Him about your problems, ask forgiveness for your weaknesses, and pray for strength to do better tomorrow, for Him to show you ways you can grow and be more useful to Him.

In Matt 5:44 Sometimes this one may be hard, but we are to pray for the very people that hurt us, why?? you may ask, well if you have anger and unforgiving in your heart, how can God forgive you.

The prayer that always starts my day is the one Jesus gave us Himself in Matt 6:9 its the prayer that He said and told us to remember and pray, Our Father, who art in Heaven, read this one, write it down, remember it, carry it in your heart.

This is the blessing of having pray in your life Matt 21:22 ask anything in my name and you will receive, When you pray for anything, you have to believe in your heart that God hears you and will keep the promises in His word.

If what you are asking is in His will He will answer, but also we have to know, if the person we are praying for has lessons to learn for them to grow, our prayer for them may not be answered over night.

Just as we have things to learn and things to go through to make us stronger other people do too,we cam pray for there lessons to be learned quickly, but we have to believe in our prayers, in our healing s, this is stressed again in James 5:15 pray and believe. Mark 11:24-25

In Luke 20 :46-47 Even though we are taught to pray the Our Father we aren't to have that our only conversation with God, its not a cover all prayer for the day. the long drawn out prayers, that are repeated every day, the same over and over are not what He wants from us.

He wants fellowship with us, in 1 Thes 5-17 He wants us to pray without ceasing, all through our days, you know I told my kids when they were small, just pretend Jesus is in your pocket, the one closest to your heart.

That any time during the day you feel you need Him, just need to talk to Him, feel scared about something, need direction in something. He is as close as your heart, we as adults need this also.

We all need to put Jesus in our pocket and have Him close to our hearts all day, always there with us, always there to talk to, always there to cry out to, and always close to just say thank you for being there for me today.

And never forget the other part of having conversation, its a art, not always easy, but we have to take time to listen, we have to set apart a special time of the day, one that is best for your schedule, if it be early in the morning or late in the evening. where you take time to listen, you will feel your answers in your heart, something will just all the sudden make since to you, or a change will be made in your life.

But God will answer your prayers, but if you don't stop long enough to listen, you may not see how He has, take time tomorrow and try something, wake up in the morning and just thank God for the day you have just been given.

Go get a piece of paper or something and write Jesus name on it, now put it in your pocket, bra, what ever you have on where it will be next to your heart, and know and believe He is that close to you all day,

After you do this awhile, you wont need the small piece of paper, you will know Hes there, you will feel His presence that close to you all day, and then you will know you have what He wants with you, you will have found fellowship with your Savior.

I hope this is going to help someone just a little ,to have a closer relationship with your Father in Heaven, to really know Him as a friend.

WHAT DO OTHER'S SEE

THIS WEEK HAS BEEN A EYE OPENER FOR ME IN SO VERY MANY WAYS, WAYS THAT I HAVE REALLY LOOKED AT MY OWN HEART, THE REASONS BEHIND OUR ACTIONS, AND ALWAYS LOOKING FOR THE BEST DEAL IN EVERYTHING WE DO AND EVERYTHING WE BUY.

HOW OFTEN HAVE WE BEEN DRIVING DOWN A ROAD OR STREET AND SEEN THE WORD FREE, MADE A U TURN AND GONE TO CHECK IT OUT, OR THE BUY ONE GET ONE FREE, GET THIS AND ONE MONTH FREE SERVICE, THE WORD FREE ALWAYS SEEMS TO STAND OUT.

SOMETIMES ITS A GOOD DEAL, BUT OFTEN TIMES YOU GET WHAT YOU PAY FOR AND END UP WITH SOMETHING THAT BREAKS IN A WEEK OR SO, BUT THE FREE THING I AM GOING TO TELL YOU ABOUT TODAY HAS A LIFETIME GUARANTEE.

WHEN WE COME TO JESUS AS A SINNER, THE SALVATION YOU RECIEVE IS FREE, JESUS DIED ON THE CROSS SO THAT YOU CAN HAVE FREE SALVATION, IT COMES WITH A LIFETIME GUARANTEE AND NEVER BREAKS, NEVER RUST, NEVER NEEDS REBOOTING, NEVER NEEDS PAINTED, PRIMED, ITS THE SAME YESTERDAY ,TODAY AND ALWAYS.

IN JOHN 8;32 THE TRUTH SHALL MAKE YO FREE, JOHN 8:36 YOU SHALL BE FREE INDEED. ROMANS 5:15 WE HAVE A FREE GIFT, NOT TO BE TAKEN LIGHTLY, BUT YOU KNOW WHAT HAS GONE THROUGH MY MIND TODAY HASNT BEEN DEALING WITH THE GIFT ITSELF, IT'S BEEN HOW WE ABUSE THE GIFT.

WHAT I SEE IS SO VERY MANY PEOPLE RUSHING TO GET THEIR FREE GIFT, SHOWING IT TO THEIR FRIENDS WHEN ITS NEW AND THEN PUTTING IT ON A SHELF TO GATHER DUST TILL THERE LAST BREATH IS NEAR, THEN THEY TAKE IT DOWN AND HOLD IT AGAIN.

THEY HAVENT LOVED THE GIFT, THEY HAVE RESPECTED THE GIFT, THEY HAVENT USED THE GIFT, JUST HAD THE PEACE OF KNOWING IT WAS THEIRS IF THEY NEEDED IT, WHEN THEY

ARE SICK THEY MAY USE IT, IF THEY ARE IN TROUBLE THEY MIGHT USE IT, BUT I ASK YOU TO SEARCH YOUR HEART, IS THIS USEING IT OR ABUSEING IT.

    IN THIS DAY AND TIME WHEN SO MANY ARE SEARCHING FOR HOPE, SEARCHING FOR REASONS TO HANG ON TO LIFE ONE MORE DAY, LOOKING FOR SOMEONE TO UNDERSTAND THEIR PAIN, TO FORGIVE THEM OF THE WRONGS THEY HAVE DONE.

    ARE THEY GOING TO SEE THIS IN YOU ? ARE THEY GOING TO SEE THIS IN ME ? DO YOU HAVE THE GIFT OF YOUR SALVATION IN YOUR HEART SO MUCH THAT OTHERS ARE ABLE TO SEE IT IN YOU, THROUGH YOU, IN YOUR WORDS AND YOUR ACTIONS.

    WE AS CHRISTIANS DONT HAVE A WORLD THAT IS FREE FROM TRIALS, IN FACT WE MAY AT TIMES HAVE MORE, FOR THE SIMPLE REASON THE DEVIL IS GOING TO TRY TO GET YOU BACK SERVING HIM, TEMPT YOU WITH THE PLEASURES YOU HAD BEFORE, WITH THE ANGER YOU HAD BEFORE, WITH THE LUST YOU HAD BEFORE.

    EVERYTIME YOU GIVE IN TO ONE OF THESE AND OTHER NON CHRISTIANS SEE IT, THEY SEE JESUS NAME DRUG THROUGH THE MUD, THE WITNESS YOU WERE SUPPOSE TO BE FOR HIM JUST GOT TARNISHED. BUT YOU HAVE A WAY TO MAKE IT RIGHT, DONT GIVE UP JUST BECAUSE YOU FAIL.

    WHEN THINGS HAPPEN AND YOU KNOW YOU HAVE SLIPPED UP, GO STRAIGHT TO GOD AND TELL HIM, ASK HIM TO FORGIVE YOU AND GIVE YOU THE STRENGTH TO OVER COME THIS THING THAT HAS STRONG HOLDS ON YOU, SOMETIMES THINGS CAN BE TAKEN THE VERY SECOND YOU TAKE JESUS IN IN YOUR HEART.

    FOR OTHERS THERE MAY BE LESSONS YOU HAVE TO LEARN IN ORDER TO BE STRONG ENOUGH TO OVERCOME THE TEMPTATIONS, ITS ALL AS PERSONAL AS YOUR FINGERPRINT, EVERYONE IS DIFFERENT AND GOD DEALS WITH EVERYONE IN DIFFERENT WAYS.

    BUT IN THE END YOU WILL HAVE THE POWER TO OVERCOME, IF YOU DONT PUT YOUR GIFT ON THE SHELF, YOU SEE THIS IS A FREE GIFT WITH A SPECIAL TOUCH, THE MORE YOU

USE IT, THE BETTER IT GETS, IT DOESNT GET WEAK OR WEAR OUT, IT GETS STRONGER THE MORE YOU USE IT.

THE MORE YOU CALL ON JESUS, THE CLOSER FRIENDSHIP YOU HAVE WITH HIM, THE MORE YOU KNOW HIM, THE MORE YOU LOVE HIM AND THE EASIER IT GETS TO ACT LIKE HIM, THINK LIKE HIM, HE BECOMES A PART OF YOU LIKE YOUR ARM OR LEG, AND IT GETS TO THE POINT YOU CANT DO ANYTHING WITHOUT HIM.

EVERY BREATH YOU BREATHE WILL HAVE HIS NAME ON IT, YOU WILL SEE THINGS WITH HIS EYES, THE EYES OF COMPASSION, YOU WILL LOVE WITH A UNCONDITIONAL LOVE, YOU WILL HAVE A HEART THAT SHARES JOY AND TEARS WITH OTHERS BECAUSE YOU WILL FEEL THERE EMOTIONS.

IT REALLY IS SUCH A COMPLEAT JOY TO HAVE JESUS IN YOUR HEART, THERE IS A PEACE THAT YOU REALLY CANT EXPLAIN, THERE IS A SAFE FEELING IN ALL SITUATIONS BECAUSE YOU KNOW HE IS RIGHT THERE WITH YOU, THERE IS NO FEAR.

CALL HIS NAME, ASK HIM TO FORGIVE YOU AND COME TAKE OVER YOUR LIFE, TO FILL YOUR HEART ALL THE WAY UP, TO GUIDE YOU IN ALL YOU DO, TO GIVE YOU THE STRENGTH TO CHANGE THE THINGS THAT HAVENT BEEN BRINGING GLORY TO HIS NAME.

TAKE JESUS OFF THE SHELF AND CARRY HIM IN YOUR POCKET, THE ONE CLOSEST TO YOUR HEART AND KEEP HIM THERE, CARRY HIM WITH YOU IN ALL YOU DO, TALK TO HIM THROUGH OUT THE DAY, SHARE YOUR THOUGHTS, FEARS AND DREAMS WITH HIM.

MY PRAYER FOR YOU ALL TODAY IS THAT IF YOU HAVE HAD JESUS UP ON YOUR SHELF, THAT YOU WILL TAKE HIM DOWN FROM THERE, DUST HIM OFF AND PUT HIM IN YOUR POCKET, RIGHT NOW, THIS VERY MINUTE, BEFORE ANYTHING ELSE GETS YOUR ATTENTION.

LET TODAY BE THE BEGINNING OF A CLOSER FRIENDSHIP WITH JESUS, ONE THAT WILL TURN INTO A LOVE AFFAIR THAT NEVER DIES, BECAUSE YOU WILL NEVER FIND ANYONE THAT

WILL LOVE YOU MORE.

DONT BE DECEIVED

     THE STUDY I AM DOING TODAY CAME ABOUT BY MISTAKE,LAST WEEK OUR PASTOR TOLD US WHAT OUR HOME WORK WOULD BE FOR OUR WEDNESDAY NIGHT STUDY,I COULD HAVE SWORN HE SAID ACTS 16, WELL IT WASNT , IT WAS 1 COR 16, BUT I STUDIED BOTH ANYWAY.
     WELL THROUGH THE STUDY I DID SO MANY THINGS CAME TO MIND..THINGS I HAD NEVER THOUGHT ABOUT AND MANY THINGS I HAD TO NOW PRAY AND ASK FORGIVENESS FOR, MY EYES HAD BEEN COVERED LIKE A SNAKE SKIN BEFORE IT SHEDS.
     THE REASON I SAY THIS IS FOR THIS REASON..WHEN WE READ ACTS 16 WE SEE THAT PAUL HAS TAKEN TIMOTHY AND THEY ARE GOING ON A JOURNEY, THEY ARE GOING WITH THE HOLY SPIRIT LEADING THEM IN EVERYTHING THEY DO,WHERE THEY GO AND WHAT THEY SAY ON THEIR WAY.
     WHEN THEY START TO GO INTO THIS ONE AREA THE SPIRIT TELLS THEM NOT TO GO THERE SO THEY GO TO A DIFFERENT AREA, AND THIS IS WHERE MY STORY STARTS,THEY HAVE WALKED THROUGH THE STREETS PREACHING AND BAPTIZING, GETTING CHURCHES STARTED.
     PEOPLE SEE THE GOOD THINGS THEY ARE DOING, THE WATCH, THEY LISTEN,THEY LEARN, BUT GOOD PEOPLE ARENT THE ONLY ONES LISTENING,IN VERSE 16 WE SEE THERE IS A WOMAN ALSO WATCHING THERE EVERY MOVE, STUDING THEM.
     SHE IS A FORTUNE TELLER,ONE THAT MAKES A LIVING READING CARDS,TELLING PEOPLE THEIR FUTURE, SHE GOES WITH THEM,AND FORTELLS THAT THEY ARE WISE MEN OF GOD, HIGH SERVENTS OF GOD..YES HER WORDS ARE GOOD,SHE IS PRETENDING TO SPEAK GOOD, BUT SHE IS DOING IT IN A WAY

THAT IT WILL APPEAR SHE IS TELLING OF THINGS SHE SEES AS A FORTUNE TELLER FOR HER GAIN.

PAUL IS LEAD BY THE HOLY SPIRIT AND CAST THE DEMON OUT OF HER, AND NOW SHE IS NO LONGER POSSESSED BY THE DEMONTIC SPIRIT. SHE IS NO LONGER ABLE TO BE USED BY THE DEVIL FOR HIS GAIN AND NOW THE TOWN IS ANGRY,THEY PUT PAUL AND TIMOTHY IN JAIL..YOU CAN READ THE REST BUT THIS IS WHERE I NEED TO SPEAK TO YOU.

YOU SEE YEARS AGO I TOO USED CARDS TO TELL PEOPLE OF THINGS TO COME, I USED ANGEL CARDS, CARDS FOR WOMEN AND WAS DOING THIS THINKING IT WAS HELPING THEM, I THOUGHT IT WAS GOOD,THE MAN I WAS MARRIED TO AT THAT TIME WOULD STUDY PEOPLE AND USE IT FOR MONEY AND CONTROL, I DIDNT CHARGE SO I THOUGHT MY WAY WAS JUST TO HELP.

YOU SEE I WAS BEING DECEIVED, AND AT THAT TIME WASNT EVEN SEEING THE SIN IN IT, IN THE STUDY I FOUND OUT THE SPIRIT THAT USES AND TAKES OVER IS IN THE GREEK CALLED THE PYTHON SPIRIT, THE LARGEST SERPENTS ON THE EARTH TODAY.

AT THE TIME I WAS DOING ALL OF THIS, MY THEN HUSBAND HAD GOT ME WHERE I WASNT AFRAID OF SNAKES ANY MORE, I WOULD HOLD THEM WHILE HE CLEANED THE CAGES, AND SOMETIMES JUST TO HOLD THEM, WHAT SORT OF SNAKES???

WE HAD LUKE, A 8 FT REDTAILED BOA, BETTY BOOP A 8 FT FEMALE REDTAILED BOA, STRIKER,A BURMISES PYTHON, 6 FT LONG, GOLDIE A GOLDEN BOA, AND A RETICULATED PYTHON 6 FT LONG, WE HAD CAGES ALL OVER OUR HOME, IN ABOUT EVERY ROOM.

THE SPIRIT OF THE SERPENT WASNT JUST IN OUR HOME IT WAS IN US. I WAS SO COVERED WITH THIS SPIRIT AND LIKE A SNAKE WHEN ITS GOING TO SHED, MY EYES WERE COVERED TO THE SIN AND DECEIPTION I WAS DOING AND I ALLOWED IT TO HAPPEN IN MY HOME.

TODAY I HAVE TO ASK FORGIVENESS FOR ALL THE PEOPLE I

LEAD ASTRAY ,HOW MANY SOULS WERE LOST DO TO THE LIES AND DECEPTION I WAS FILLING THEM WITH,HOW MANY SOULS WENT TO HELL BECAUSE I TOLD THEM LIES NOT TRUTH.

 THE PAIN I FELT WAS SO AWFUL, WHAT I WANT TO SHARE TODAY IS THIS, WE HAVE TO OPEN OUR EYES TO WHAT SIN REALLY IS, IT CAN BE SUGAR COATED SO EASY AND MADE TO LOOK SO INNOCENT, WE HAVE TO SEE WHEN YOU GO TO A FORTUNE TELLER WHAT YOU ARE DOING IS ASKING THE DEVIL TO TELL YOU WHAT YOUR FUTURE IS.

 YOU ARE PAYING THE DEVIL FOR THE SIN AND NOW YOU DONT HAVE MONEY FOR YOUR TITHE AT CHURCH, YES THERE ARE CHRISTIANS THAT FOR FUN WILL GO HAVE THEIR FORTUNES READ. THEY MAY GO OUT OF TOWN SO THEIR FRIENDS DONT FIND OUT .. BUT THEY DO.

 BUT THE HOPE WE HAVE IS THIS, LIKE THE SNAKE THAT SHEDS IT SKIN AND IS NEW, SO ARE WE WHEN WE TAKE CHRIST AS OUR SAVIOR,WE SHED THAT OLD SKIN AND HAVE A NEW LIFE,WE GROW AND FROM TIME TO TIME HAVE TO SHED SOME MORE.

 AS WE KEEP GROWING, WE HAVE TO KEEP SHEDDING, FOR JUST AS THE SNAKE, IF WE HAVE SOMETHING WRONG AND WE DONT SHED ANY MORE WE DIE, DONT BE LIKE I WAS AND NOT SEE SIN FOR WHAT IT REALLY IS, DONT SUGAR COAT YOUR SIN SO IT DOESNT LOOK AS BAD, THATS WHAT YOU DO IF YOU FIND REASONS WHY YOU DO SOMETHING AND YOU KNOW ITS NOT RIGHT,

 MY PRAYER TODAY IS THAT THIS HAS OPENED SOMEONES EYES, SOMETIMES ITS ME THAT HAS TO SEE THINGS IN A DIFFERENT WAY..SOMETIMES ITS MY EYES THAT HAVE TO BE OPENED, I AM FAR FROM PERFECT AND I TOO GROW EACH TIME I WRITE A BIBLESTUDY FOR YOU.

 I PRAY FOR ALL MY READERS DAILY AND PRAY NOW THAT THIS HAS HELPED SOMEONE, EVEN IF ITS JUST ONE PERSON OUT OF THE HUNDREDS OUT THERE, THIS WAS FOR YOU....AND FOR ME.. I LOVE YOU ALL AND MAY GOD ALWAYS GUIDE AND PROTECT..HEAL AND COMFORT YOU.

REAL LIFE, OUR DAYS ARE NOT PART OF A PROMISE.

scriptures Psalm 91/ 1 John 5:18 / Ephesians 6:16 / 2 Peter 1:2-4/ Mark 11:22-24/ and James 3:1-12

Oh the power of the Psalms to calm the spirit, over the last few weeks I have been so consumed with fear for the future and what it could hold for my children and myself.

Friends would try to comfort and offer prayer and the pain was still over taking me daily, but then someone said get into the word, there you will find your answers and guess what I did.

I have found that in all things God will get the glory, through everything we go through, we have a message to share, we try so hard to protect our loved ones that we fail to see reality, I was filled with so much fear of the word Army it was like they said cancer to me.

But you know what, I did a little research, and did you know more people are killed in 6 months here in Missouri on our roads, drive by's, murders than in 6 months in the war. If you have a child, husband, friend that wants to be a police officer, fireman. Security guard at prison, they are all in danger at every hour.

So does that mean we live in fear everyday, do we allow it to consume our thoughts to the point we make ourselves sick, or do we call out to God and trust Him with our lives and the lives of our loved ones.

I realized yesterday even if for some reason Tim cant get in the army, his life is not promised tomorrow, we have to claim protection daily and claim the promise we have in the word.

Lets read Psalm 91 , how many have claimed this one and really found peace through a situation_____

    I have felt such peace for the first time in a long time, and now when I cry its because I know God has a promise He is keeping to me, I have found that no matter how strong you may want to be and how much time you spend in prayer, the devil will find a soft spot and keep attacking it till he makes a hole he can send his demons into.

    This has become really real , he couldn't attack so much when awake but would fill my dream time with night mares that the fear would be there as soon as I awoke.

    So now I pray for God to place a shield over my mind and bind the dreams and fear and thank him for hearing me, and fall asleep in prayer

In 1 John 5:18 We know that anyone born of God does not continue to sin; the One who was born of God keeps them safe, and the evil one cannot harm them.

Eph 6:16 In addition to all this, take up the shield of faith, with which you can extinguish all the flaming arrows of the evil one.

2 Peter 1:1-4

Grace and peace be yours in abundance through the knowledge of God and of Jesus our Lord.

2Pe 1:3 His divine power has given us everything we need for a Godly life through our knowledge of him who called us by his own glory and goodness.

2Pe 1:4 Through these he has given us his very great and precious promises, so that through them you may participate in the divine nature, having escaped the corruption in the world caused by evil desires.

    God has given us the tools to fight fear in His very word, and no matter how we are being attacked we have a shield, we have to see this shield in our mind, visualize it, feel it, know its there with out any doubt and place it around your loved ones and yourselves.

    We have to see the closer we get to being what God has called us to be, the closer we get to being transformed into that butterfly, the more we are going to be plagued with things to destroy it.

But instead of seeing it in fear we need to see these attacks in power , see that if we weren't in Gods will doing what God called us to do, the devil would be leaving us alone.

can you see attacks getting stronger over the last few months_____

I know for me it has been 10 times more since I quit smoking, its like the devil really got ticked off at me, it has been one thing after another to see if he could get me weak enough to start back up.

But God took that desire away and the devil cant make it come back cause he isn't that strong. I know that no matter what happens in my life I will never pick cigarettes for my comfort.

I have seen so many of my family and friends going through so many things lately that I know they are being attacked so hard, but I also see a strength in numbers.

When we have our friends pray for us and keep us lifted up daily we are stronger, our eyes are more open to seeing where the weak spots are in our lives and then we can fight it.

James 3:1-12

1 Not many of you should presume to be teachers, my brothers and sisters, because you know that we who teach will be judged more strictly.

Jas 3:2 We all stumble in many ways. Those who are never at fault in what they say are perfect, able to keep their whole body in check.

Jas 3:3 When we put bits into the mouths of horses to make them obey us, we can turn the whole animal.

Jas 3:4 Or take ships as an example. Although they are so large and are driven by strong winds, they are steered by a very small rudder wherever the pilot wants to go.

Jas 3:5 Likewise, the tongue is a small part of the body, but it makes great boasts. Consider what a great forest is set on fire by a small spark.

Jas 3:6 The tongue also is a fire, a world of evil among the parts of the body. It corrupts the whole person, sets the whole course of one's life on fire, and is itself set on fire by hell.

Jas 3:7 All kinds of animals, birds, reptiles and sea creatures are being tamed and have been tamed by human beings,

Jas 3:8 but no one can tame the tongue. It is a restless evil, full of deadly poison.

Jas 3:9 With the tongue we praise our Lord and Father, and with it we curse human beings, who have been made in God's likeness.

Jas 3:10 Out of the same mouth come praise and cursing. My brothers and sisters, this should not be.

Jas 3:11 Can both fresh water and salt water flow from the same spring?

Jas 3:12 My brothers and sisters, can a fig tree bear olives, or a grapevine bear figs? Neither can a salt spring produce fresh water.

The power of the spoken word is so strong, do you realizes when you say, what if this, what if that, there going to make them do this or that, you are claiming that over them, I have to remember that daily, and have had so many friends rebuke my words I have said in fear , and I thank you right now for that.

(3) what are some ways we can have more control over what comes out of our mouth._____

You know one thing that has happened for me personally I had always prayed for my country and the people serving, but until it became reality in my life, I couldn't share what every parent is going through, the things we go through in life are "life lessons" and what we learn we can help others going through it, but how can we be used to help others if we don't learn to trust, we have to have that in our hearts and mind before God can use us to help others.

I really think as the days and months ahead are coming we need to really keep each other lifted up in prayer a lot more, with stronger prayers, more intense prayer times, for the church, pastor, leaders, our families, our home life, our health, to place a shield of protection around our friends daily.

When we are being attacked call someone fast and get on prayer chain, even on the little things, we really need to become stronger prayer warriors for each other, now more than ever.

lets share some areas now that need to be daily things for each other

Psa 46:1 God is our refuge and strength, an ever-present help in trouble.

Psa 46:2 Therefore we will not fear, though the earth give way and the mountains fall into the heart of the sea,

Psa 46:3 though its waters roar and foam and the mountains quake with their surging.

Psa 46:4 There is a river whose streams make glad the city of God, the holy place where the Most High dwells.

Psa 46:5 God is within her, she will not fall; God will help her at break of day.

Psa 46:6 Nations are in uproar, kingdoms fall; he lifts his voice, the earth melts.

Psa 46:7 The Lord Almighty is with us; the God of Jacob is our fortress.

Psa 46:8 Come and see what the Lord has done, the desolation's he has brought on the earth.

Psa 46:9 He makes wars cease to the ends of the earth. He breaks the bow and shatters the spear; he burns the shields with fire.

Psa 46:10 "Be still, and know that I am God; I will be exalted among the nations, I will be exalted in the earth."

Psa 46:11 The Lord Almighty is with us; the God of Jacob is our fortress.

Psa 56:1 Be merciful to me, my God, for my enemies are in hot pursuit; all day long they press their attack.

Psa 56:2 My adversaries pursue me all day long; in their pride many are attacking me.

Psa 56:3 When I am afraid, I put my trust in you.

Psa 56:4 In God, whose word I praise-- in God I trust and am not afraid. What can mere mortals do to me?

Psa 56:5 All day long they twist my words; all their schemes are for my ruin.

Psa 56:6 They conspire, they lurk, they watch my steps, hoping to take my life.

Psa 56:7 Because of their wickedness do not let them escape; in your anger, God, bring the nations down.

Psa 56:8 Record my misery; list my tears on your scroll-- are they not in your record?

Psa 56:9 Then my enemies will turn back when I call for help. By this I will know that God is for me.

Psa 56:10 In God, whose word I praise, in the Lord, whose word I praise--

Psa 56:11 in God I trust and am not afraid. What can mere human beings do to me?

Psa 56:12 I am under vows to you, my God; I will present my thank offerings to you.

Psa 56:13 For you have delivered me from death and my feet from stumbling, that I may walk before God in the light of life.

As we have read these out loud, lets also claim them in our spirits, and take these words home with us in our hearts, our protection, comfort, and peace can only come from fellowship with our savior.

" GOD"S HEALTHCARE PLAN "

scriptures

leprosy healed, Leviticus 14:1-57 through obedience / 2 Kings 5:1-14/ blindness healed Isaiah 35:5-6 / matt 9:27-31 / healing Matt 10:1 / Acts 3:11-20 / faith lacked Mark 6:4-6 / healing emerged Luke 6:19 / prayer for sick James 5: 13-15/ rebuked doubt Matt 14:31 / doubt hinders sight(spiritual) matt 6:223/ divine immunity Exodus 15:26 /Deuteronomy 7:15/ protection / numbers22:12/ Isaiah 43:1-2 / Psalm 5:11

With so much thought on our health care and about our future, so many people are starting to live in fear, in fear of the dreaded "what ifs illness", this disease if left untreated can and and will cause your death.

The first sign of the disease is worry, then fear, then sleeplessness, lack of appetite, diarrhea, depression, isolation and heart disease most of the time will develop in later stages.

The death comes because if you allow all of these things to control you you will die of lack of faith, and that will be the worst part of the what if's disease.

So how do we protect ourselves from this, well it just so happens I found the medical book on how to treat this very thing, its called the bible.

(1)how many of you are having any signs of this illness right now?

---

ok now lets find the steps to the cure,In the scriptures there are 3 things you must have to find the cure and keep it, the first pill is FAITH, second pill BELIEVE, and the third pill is TRUST.

THOSE THREE PILLS CAN AND WILL SAVE YOUR LIFE

ok now where do we get these and how do we keep them, we have to see proof that they really work, ok lets go to 2 kings 5:1-14 Now Naaman was commander of the army of the king of Aram. He was a great man in the sight of his master and highly regarded, because through him the Lord had given victory to Aram. He was a valiant soldier, but he had leprosy.

2Ki 5:2 Now bands of raiders from Aram had gone out and had taken captive a young girl from Israel, and she served Naaman's wife.

2Ki 5:3 She said to her mistress, "If only my master would see the prophet who is in Samaria! He would cure him of his leprosy."

2Ki 5:4 Naaman went to his master and told him what the girl from Israel had said.

2Ki 5:5 "By all means, go," the king of Aram replied. "I will send a letter to the king of Israel." So Naaman left, taking with him ten talents of silver, six thousand shekels of gold and ten sets of clothing.

2Ki 5:6 The letter that he took to the king of Israel read: "With this letter I am sending my servant Naaman to you so that you may cure him of his leprosy."

2Ki 5:7 As soon as the king of Israel read the letter, he tore his robes and said, "Am I God? Can I kill and bring back to life? Why does this fellow send someone to me to be cured of his leprosy? See how he is trying to pick a quarrel with me!"

2Ki 5:8 When Elisha the man of God heard that the king of Israel had torn his robes, he sent him this message: "Why have you torn your robes? Have the man come to me and he will know that there is a prophet in Israel."

2Ki 5:9 So Naaman went with his horses and chariots and stopped at the door of Elisha's house.

2Ki 5:10 Elisha sent a messenger to say to him, "Go, wash yourself seven times in the Jordan, and your flesh will be restored and you will be cleansed."

2Ki 5:11 But Naaman went away angry and said, "I thought that he would surely come out to me and stand and call on the name of the Lord his God, wave his hand over the spot and cure me of my leprosy.

2Ki 5:12 Are not Abana and Pharpar, the rivers of Damascus, better than all the waters of Israel? Couldn't I wash in them and be cleansed?" So he turned and went off in a rage.

2Ki 5:13 Naaman's servants went to him and said, "My father, if the prophet had told you to do some great thing, would you not have done it? How much more, then, when he tells you, 'Wash and be cleansed'!"

2Ki 5:14 So he went down and dipped himself in the Jordan seven times, as the man of God had told him, and his flesh was restored and became clean like that of a young boy.

In Lev 14:1-57 BEFORE JESUS TIME IS WAS HEALED THROUGH OBEDIANCE , THEY FOLLOWED WHAT GOD HAD TOLD MOSES .WITH FAITH AND BELIEF.

in these two stories we find that leprosy is healed by what, the pill of faith and belief, we can look at Isaiah 35: 5-6, Then will the eyes of the blind be opened and the ears of the deaf unstopped.

Then will the lame leap like a deer, and the mute tongue shout for joy. Water will gush forth in the wilderness and streams in the desert.

Matt 10:1, Jesus called his twelve disciples to him and gave them authority to drive out evil spirits and to heal every disease and sickness.

Luke 6:19 *who had come to hear him and to be healed of their diseases. Those troubled by evil spirits were cured,*

Luk 6:19 and the people all tried to touch him, because power was coming from him and healing them all.

in all of these scriptures we see the one thing all these people shared was the 3 little pills.

So how are we going to find these, we have to know in all of our being that the word is true, we have to feel it so deep in our spirit that it really is a part of you.

*2. do you feel like you have that faith yet that belief, that trust.*_____

we need a insurance policy we can really trust to take us the rest of our lives, one that will hold up through all the new laws our government may have for us.

We have to see people may let us down but God never will, and he has promised us this from the very beginning., let us go over these scriptures this evening and really read them,

numbers 22:12/psalm 5:11/psalm 32:7/Isaiah 43:1-2/ 1 peter 1:3-4

we have to see that as children of God the King of all Kings we really are His princesses. numbers 22:12 But God said to Balaam, "Do not go with them. You must not put a curse on those people, because they are blessed."

we are all blessed and under His protection, psalm 5 :11 But let all who take refuge in you be glad; let them ever sing for joy. Spread your protection over them, that those who love your name may rejoice in you./Psalm 32:7.You are my hiding place; you will protect me from trouble and surround me with songs of deliverance., Isaiah 43:1-2

But now, this is what the Lord says-- he who created you, Jacob, he who formed you, Israel: "Do not fear, for I have redeemed you; I have summoned you by name; you are mine. Isaiah 43:1-2

When you pass through the waters, I will be with you; and when you pass through the rivers, they will not sweep over you. When you walk through the fire, you will not be burned; the flames will not set you ablaze.

1 Peter 1: 3-4 Praise be to the God and Father of our Lord Jesus Christ! In his great mercy he has given us new birth into a living hope through the resurrection of Jesus Christ from the dead,

1Pe 1:4 and into an inheritance that can never perish, spoil or fade. This inheritance is kept in heaven for you,

We have to always feel in our hearts we belong to the king of kings, how much would you go out on a limb to help your child or your grandchild, we have to see God loves you 100 times more than you could ever love yours, He has a love we can only imagine.

To get the insurance policy we are talking about is so easy, and the best part is you never have to pay premiums, its a one time fee that is just as easy as a prayer, when we ask Jesus to be lord of our lives that policy came with it free of charge.

But we have to watch out for a few things that can take the strength out of it, it will only work if we keep it up to date, we have to check it daily, are we keeping the bugs of doubt from eating at it,, it will eat away just like termites eat away at wood, the beam that was strong will fall apart like dust if the bugs aren't kept in control .

The things that will keep a healing from manifesting, are doubt, forgiveness, anger, and sin, if any of these things are in your life they have to be dealt with and prayed for, get delivered from these and watch the manifestation take place. The healing will be there ready to bloom like a flower.

What are some areas you would want us to keep in prayer for each other, you can share or just a personal prayer, God knows and we don't have to know the details.

what are some answered prayers of healing you know about,

 THINK OF SOME WAYS WE CAN HELP EACH OTHER WITH THE HEALTH CARE PLAN GOD HAS FOR US.

DO YOU KNOW OF SOMEONE IN PAIN, PRAY, HAVE A ILLNESS PRAY, THAT IS HOW WE CAN KEEP OUR PLANS IN THE ACTIVE FILE,lets keep each other always lifted up in prayers,have a blessed week.

SCAR'S CAN BE BEAUTIFUL

    Never be ashamed of the scars that life has left you with, A scar means the hurt is over, the wound is closed, you endured the pain and God has healed you.............you know when I saw this as a post on my face book page, I really started to think about what it said.

Some times we think of the situation that made the scar, and think.. man that's

 a ugly thing...yes ugly things make scars, bad things make scars, but as the wound heals the pain is remembered less and less.

    When my children were born the pain was really bad, I refused pain killers for the health and love of my babies. but as soon as they were born the pain wasn't as bad any more. and over time it was forgotten.

    Same is the pain that has made the scars in your life. So many times in life we have to go through things to grow, painful at the time we go through them but as we heal we get stronger, have you ever really looked at a scar, it thicker skin, stronger than it was before.

    That is how you are inside when you make it through a situation that at the time seems to big, but you stand firm, plant your feet and keep saying to yourself..I know this is big God and I know I will be stronger from this. you WILLLL get the glory from this, give me the strength and wisdom to get through it and learn from this and be the person that can help someone else that I may come across later in life going through what I am right now.

    A few times in my life I have been very abused from the man in my life, my husbands, one was emotional, one was verbal and one physical. in all of them the emotional was the hardest to get over, the pain from the others went away, but it seemed emotional ones left the deepest scars.

The emotional ones hurt the heart, self worth, self respect, and left a scar that went into my other relationships. a fear, lack of trust,it really made it hard to love anyone.

(But God)

I was able to find a man in church that knew the pain as I had, he had been the one hurt and he and I were able to grow together and help heal each other from our lessons learned. I was able to reach out to girl that was raped by being able to say I know how you are feeling, I have been there, I have been able to give God the glory for the pain by reaching out to others that are going through the things I had to grow through.

When you are able to look in there eyes and say I know how you feel and they know you really do understand because you went through it too, you can reach a person no one else can.

God will make a way when there seems no way. open a door when there doesn't seem to be one,if we leave the situation in His hands and listen when He speaks to your heart.

Don't let the pain turn you into something ugly, allow the pain to make you a creation God can use to help others. in that God will get the glory.

KNOWING OUR LIMITS

YOU KNOW THIS STUDY IS COMING ABOUT IN A REALLY STRANGE WAY TONIGHT, BUT WHEN YOU ASK GOD TO SHOW YOU ANSWERS, SOMETIMES THIS IS THE WAY IT HAPPENS.

YOU SEE SO MANY THINGS HAVE BEEN POURING INTO MY SPIRIT OVER THE LAST FEW DAYS, WEEKS AND SOMETHING OVER A MONTH, SOME THINGS HAVE BEEN CONFIRMED SOME THINGS I AM STILL IN MUCH PRAYER ABOUT.
I KNOW MANY OF YOU ALREADY KNOW ABOUT THE AREA I AM SPEAKING ABOUT, ABOUT THE SHELTER FOR THE HOMELESS THAT TOM AND I WANT TO START UP SOMEPLACE IN THE NEXT FEW YEARS.

ITS A CALLING THAT IS VERY STRONG AND I HAVE BEEN DOING RESEARCH EVERY DAY, EVENING, PLANNING, SPEAKING TO DIFFERENT PEOPLE AND GETTING IDEAS.

I FELT WITH ALL THAT WAS IN ME THIS PASSION TO STEP OUT RIGHT NOW, IT COULDNT BE THAT HARD...BUT YOU KNOW WHAT I LEARNED.

Rom 1:1 I, Paul, am a devoted slave (SERVENT)of Jesus Christ on assignment, authorized as an apostle to proclaim God's words and acts. I write this letter to all the Christians in Rome, God's friends.
WE ARE CALLED FIRST TO BE A SERVENT.
TOM ASKED ME TONIGHT, HAVE YOU EVER WORKED IN A SOUP KITCHEN BEFORE? I SAID NO WHY, WELL MAYBE YOU NEED TO START OUT WITH VOLUNTEER THINGS AND LEARN FROM PEOPLE THAT ARE DOING IT.
BUT THAT ISNT A SHELTER , THATS JUST A MEAL. BUT WAIT, ISNT THAT WHAT THE SCRIPTURE HAD JUST SAID, BE A SERVENT FIRST, SO WITH ALL THE THINGS PASTOR TALKED TO ME ABOUT AND NOW TOM TELLS ME THIS, AND THE SCRIPTURES BACK IT ALL UP.IT ALL IS FALLING INTO PLACE.

Isa 6:8 Then I heard the voice of the Lord saying, "Whom shall I send? And who will go for us?" And I said, "Here am I. Send me!"
Isa 6:9 He said, "Go and tell this people: "'Be ever hearing, but never understanding; be ever seeing, but never perceiving.'LOOK AT VERSE 10 AND 11

YOU CAN HAVE THE CALLING SO VERY STRONG TO REACH OUT IN A AREA, BUT WE HAVE TO ALWAYS SEARCH THE SCRIPTURES FIRST.
HOMELESSNESS HAS BEEN THERE SINCE THE DAYS OF MOSES.

Job 24:3 They rip off the poor and exploit the unfortunate,
Job 24:4 Push the helpless into the ditch, bully the weak so that they fear for their lives.
Job 24:5 The poor, like stray dogs and cats, scavenge for food in back alleys.
Job 24:6 They sort through the garbage of the rich, eke out survival on handouts.
Job 24:7 Homeless, they shiver through cold nights on the street; they've no place to lay their heads.
Job 24:8 Exposed to the weather, wet and frozen, they huddle in makeshift shelters.
THIS IS IN OUR CITIES NOW
Psa 107:3 Then rounded you up from all over the place, from the four winds, from the seven seas.
Psa 107:4 Some of you wandered for years in the desert, looking but not finding a good place to live,
Even Jesus was homeless Luk 9:58 Jesus replied, "Foxes have holes and birds have nests, but the Son of Man has no place to lay his head."
HOW MANY OF YOU HAVE SEEN A HOMELESS PERSON ON THE STREET HERE OR IN THE CITY, WHAT WAS YOUR HONEST FIRST THOUGHT_____-
YOU HAVE TO LOOK AT THEM THE SAME WAY JESUS WOULD, BUT NOW DAYS YOU ALSO HAVE TO BE CAREFUL AND NOT BE TO TRUSTING, IT CAN PLACE YOU IN DANGER IF YOU SEE EVERYONE AS A PERSON IN NEED AND NOT A PERSON THAT MAY HAVE A HARD HEART THAT WOULD WANT TO DO YOU HARM.
SOMETIMES WE HAVE HALF HEARTED WORKERS TOO, THEY HAVE BEEN AROUND FOR A LONG TIME ALSO. Dan 11:34 When the testing is intense, they'll get some help, but not much. Many of the helpers will be halfhearted at best.

YOU KNOW WE ARE ALL CALLED TO REACH OUT TO PEOPLE IN NEED, IT IS IN ALL OF OUR HEARTS, JUST IN DIFFERENT DEGREES. 1Co 3:6 I planted the seed, Apollos watered the plants, but God made you grow.

1Co 3:7 It's not the one who plants or the one who waters who is at the center of this process but God, who makes things grow.

1Co 3:8 Planting and watering are menial servant jobs at minimum wages.

1Co 3:9 What makes them worth doing is the God we are serving. You happen to be God's field in which we are working. Or, to put it another way, you are God's house.

WE ALL HAVE A JOB WE ARE CALLED TO DO, AND DO IT TO OUR VERY BEST, WE ALL HAVE SEEDS TO PLANT, SOME ARE WITH PRAYERS, SOME ARE WITH KIND WORDS OR ACTIONS, AND SOME ARE AS SERVENTS, TO THE VERY PEOPLE WE MAY HAVE LOOKED DOWN ON BEFORE WE WERE SAVED AND ASKED GOD TO USE US. Col 1:24 I want you to know how glad I am that it's me sitting here in this jail and not you. There's a lot of suffering to be entered into in this world--the kind of suffering Christ takes on. I welcome the chance to take my share in the church's part of that suffering.

Col 1:25 When I became a servant in this church, I experienced this suffering as a sheer gift, God's way of helping me serve you, laying out the whole truth.

Col 1:26 This mystery has been kept in the dark for a long time, but now it's out in the open.

Col 1:27 God wanted everyone, not just Jews, to know this rich and glorious secret inside and out, regardless of their background, regardless of their religious standing. The mystery in a nutshell is just this: Christ is in you, therefore you can look forward to sharing in God's glory. It's that simple. That is the substance of our Message.

Col 1:28 We preach Christ, warning people not to add to the Message. We teach in a spirit of profound common sense so that we can bring each person to maturity. To be mature is to be basic. Christ! No more, no less.

Col 1:29 That's what I'm working so hard at day after day, year after year, doing my best with the energy God so generously gives me.
WHAT ARE SOME THINGS YOU SEE DIFFERENT NOW THAT YOU USED TO SEE SO DIFFERENT BEFORE YOU WERE SAVED,
_____

CAN YOU SHARE SOME THINGS THAT HAVE BEEN LESSONS IN YOUR LIFE THAT MAY HELP SOMEONE GOING THROUGH IT NOW OR IN THE FUTURE._____
___

2Ti 4:2 so proclaim the Message with intensity; keep on your watch. Challenge, warn, and urge your people. Don't ever quit. Just keep it simple.

2Ti 4:3 You're going to find that there will be times when people will have no stomach for solid teaching, but will fill up on spiritual junk food--catchy opinions that tickle their fancy.

2Ti 4:4 They'll turn their backs on truth and chase mirages.

2Ti 4:5 But you--keep your eye on what you're doing; accept the hard times along with the good; keep the Message alive; do a thorough job as God's servant.

ONE THING THAT IS VERY IMPORTANT, WE HAVE TO REMEMBER

NOT TO PREACH TO PEOPLE THAT ARE HURT, YOU CAN DO MORE DAMAGE THAN GOOD, WE NEED TO SPEAK OF LOVE NOT LESSONS THEY NEED TO LEARN, YOU CAN SHARE YOUR LESSONS WITH A LOVING WAY THAT WILL SHOW HOW GOD WAS WITH YOU AND HE USED THAT LESSON TO REACH THEM.

Isa 12:4 And as you do it, you'll say, "Give thanks to GOD. Call out his name. Ask him anything! Shout to the nations, tell them what he's done, spread the news of his great reputation!

Isa 12:5 "Sing praise-songs to GOD. He's done it all! Let the whole earth know what he's done!

Isa 45:22 So turn to me and be helped--saved!-- everyone, whoever and wherever you are. I am GOD, the only God there is, the one and only.

33 "'Those who keep their heads on straight will teach the crowds right from wrong by their example. They'll be put to severe testing for a season: some killed, some burned, some exiled, some robbed.
Rom 15:30 I have one request, dear friends: Pray for me. Pray strenuously with and for me--to God the Father, through the power of our Master Jesus, through the love of the Spirit--
Rom 15:31 that I will be delivered from the lions' den of unbelievers in Judea. Pray also that my relief offering to the Jerusalem Christians will be accepted in the spirit in which it is given.
Rom 15:32 Then, God willing, I'll be on my way to you with a light and eager heart, looking forward to being refreshed by your company.
YOU KNOW WE HAVE TO REALLY START MAKING A POINT TO PRAY FOR PEOPLE WE KNOW THAT ARE DOING A MINISTRY SOMEPLACE, IN DIFFERENT AREAS, SOMETIMES I KNOW FOR ME PERSONALLY I FORGET THEM, I PRAY FOR PEOPLE AND THINGS I SEE ,BUT THEY ARE OUT OF SIGHT AND NOT REMEMBERD AS MUCH, OH WHEN WE HAVE REVIVAL I LIFT THEM UP FOR A FEW WEEKS AFTER AND THEN I START SLIPPING UP AND MAYBE ONCE AWEEK OR MONTH. WE REALLY NEED TO MAKE A PRAYER FOR MINISTRIES LIST AND START DOING THIS DAILY WITH OUR OTHER ONES.
Co 3:5 Who do you think Paul is, anyway? Or Apollos, for that matter? Servants, both of us--servants who waited on you as you gradually learned to entrust your lives to our mutual Master. We each carried out our servant assignment.
WE ARE ALL SERVENTS, AND NO MATTER WHAT WE DO IN WHAT AREA, WHEN WE ARE MINISTERING TO PEOPLE WITH A REAL LOVE IN OUR HEART, REACHING OUT WITH COMPASSION , PUTTING OURSELVES SECOND AT TIMES IF IT WILL HELP SOMEONE, WE ARE BEING SERVENTS. WE HAVE NO RIGHT TO JUDGE THE REASONS FOR SOMEONE BEING ON THE STREETS, ONLY TO REACH OUT IN A WAY TO SHOW THEM JESUS LOVE THROUGH OUR ACTIONS. 2Ti 4:1 I can't impress this on you too strongly. God is looking over your shoulder. Christ himself is the Judge, with the final say on everyone, living and dead. He is about to break into the open with his rule.

REMOVING YOUR VEIL

Our scriptures are going to be from Daniel chapter 10 this is one we really don"t use to much, but today there is a message I was made aware of, and I want to share it with you.

Last night at church the study was dealing with fasting and prayer for closer vision of what God has for your life, but as pastor was speaking I had something come to me with this same scripture.

In verse 8 we see how Daniel has after he had been fasting for 3 weeks, was very weak the strength drained from him, and at this time when he was very weak he has a vision and a angel comes to him, the angel tells him to fear not and to listen.

Then the angel told him what was ahead of him and how to stay strong and fear not and he would be shown the truth. But what came to my mind was how often do we have a time of fasting and prayer we feel so close to our savior and are willing to listen and be shown, and something really awful happens.

A family member gets hurt, or sick, something happens to your job or your car, or maybe all the above, through all these things happening a veil goes up over your eyes, the devil has placed a veil of sadness, worry, anger, over your eyes.

Why ? So you miss your vision, God was getting ready to show you something great and the devil knew this, so his plan was to put road blocks in the way, to cover your eyes with other things so you will miss it.

You had fasted and your spirit was now weak, and humble enough to hear God and listen to what He was getting ready to tell you, but even if at that time you may feel weak, you have to remain strong in your soul.

Keep your eyes open to the things around you and know when things start happening where they are coming from, pray that God will keep your eyes open to these things and trust you see what is going on too and have it in control.

We have to get to the point that we know with all that is in us that the world and all that is in it is also in Gods hands, when the world sometimes looks so bad it gets over whelming , that is because we only have human eyes to see the picture.

But God already has a plan in place to solve it and is just waiting for our hearts to be ready so He can use us.

When we fast we get our hearts and mind in Gods will, His actions can now take place with us, but if the devil can place a veil over your eyes just long enough, you will miss it and god has to start all over, and you are left with the feeling that fasting really doesn't work, so the devil wins 2 victory's.

So you ask how do we keep this veil from forming, all you have to do is know its out there, pray for your eyes to be open to see it and when things start happening that would normally upset you, praise God and say I KNOW you are bigger than this and I leave this situation in your hands, stay strong in knowing what is happening and also knowing if the devil is going to try to steal your joy and your knowledge that God is getting ready to show you something really big, you are being prepared for a plan God has had for you for so long but your heart wasn't in the right place, now you are ready and have prepared your body to be a vessel for God to use, I can relate to this so well for years ago I had decided to really follow Gods will in my life.

It was at that point my marriage fell apart, do to cheating, there was a divorce and a man came into my life that I know was placed there by the devil himself, I had a veil of deception over my eyes for 10 years and God couldn't reach me.

It wasn't till that person was out of my life, through the strength God gave me to run away from them, that I could become what He had created me to be, I had a veil over my eyes so thick I couldn't see all the lies I was being fed.

I cant go back and change anything in my past, but I can share with you these things so your eyes will be open, you will have a warning of what to watch for and be strong enough to cast them off when they come.

Don't lose your vision, stand strong as Daniel, hold fast to what you know in your heart to be of God and ALWAYS remember if it isn't good, just and pure it IS NOT of God, see things for what they are and where they really come from.

My prayer for you today is that the veil will fall at your feet, and not be able to cover your eyes, that the truth will truly set you free, free to see your vision and to follow it. Be blessed and May God shine all His love on you,

THE FALLING OF ANGELS

THE FALLING OF ANGELS.. YOU THINK ABOUT SATAN AND HIS ANGELS, BUT THAT ISN'T WHAT I WANT TO TALK ABOUT TODAY, ITS THE FALLING OF ANGELS TODAY AND IN THE WORLD NOW.

HOW MANY PEOPLE DO YOU KNOW IN YOUR LIFE THAT ARE JUST SO SWEET, CAREING, PRAYERFUL, AND WOULD DO ANYTHING TO HELP ANYONE, HOW MANY TIMES HAVE YOU SAID THEY ARE JUST A ANGEL, A SWEET SPIRIT.

AT THAT TIME IN THEIR LIFE THEY ARE SO STRONG IN THEIR FAITH, YOU SEE THEM AND THINK THEY CAN HANDLE ANYTHING LIFE THROWS AT THEM,AND COME OUT GLORIOUS AND STRONG.

BUT YOU KNOW WHAT, EVEN THE VERY STRONGEST IN THEIR FAITH CAN HAVE WEAK MOMENTS, THEY HAVE PAIN SO GREAT IN THEIR LIVES THAT THEIR SPIRIT IS WEAKENED AND THEY HAVE A OPEN DOOR THAT SATAN CAN SLITHER INTO.

WE SEE SO MANY TIME IN THE BIBLE, STORIES OF PEOPLE THAT HAD WEAK MOMENTS, DAVID,PAUL,THOMAS,PETER, THEY FELL SHORT OF WHAT GOD HAD PLANED FOR THEM AND THEY DID THINGS THAT CAUSED GOD SO MUCH PAIN.

BUT GOD NEVER GAVE UP ON THEM, NEVER LEFT THEM AND NEVER FORSAKED THEM, THEY TURNED AWAY FROM GODS WILL, HE NEVER TURNED AWAY FROM THEM AND WAS ALWAYS THERE WAITING WITH OPEN ARMS FOR THEM TO COME BACK TO SERVEING AND BE USED FOR HIS GLORY.

THE BIGGEST VICTORY THE DEVIL GETS IS WHEN HE CAN ATTACT A CHURCH LEADER, A STRONG CHRISTIAN, A NEW CHRISTIAN, ANY BELIEVER THAT HE FEELS WAS TAKEN AWAY FROM SERVEING HIM.

YOU HAVE CHRISTIANS THAT MAY HAVE GONE THROUGH A DIVORCE, OR THE LOSS OF A LOVED ONE, THEY FEEL

BITTER, ANGER, AND SO ALONE, SO THEY LET THEIR FRIENDS SAY COME ON..LETS GET YOU OUT OF THE HOUSE AWHILE.
THEN THE DEVIL SITS BACK AND WAIT'S... HIS DOOR WILL OPEN SOON, YOU SHARE YOUR PAIN WITH THOSE FRIENDS, THEY PUT A DRINK IN FRONT OF YOU, IT HAS A SWEET NAME SO IT ISNT THAT BAD.

AND SOON THAT SWEET NAMED DRINK BECOMES YOUR FRIEND, THE DOOR IS NOW OPEN AND NOW THE DEVIL CAN START TO WORK ON YOU, TO DO MORE AND MORE THINGS THAT WILL PULL YOU AWAY FROM YOUR CHRISTIAN FRIENDS, THE ONES THAT WOULD HAVE HELPED YOU STAY STRONG.

NOW YOU GO OUT ON THE WEEK ENDS WITH THOSE FRIENDS, GETTING FARTHER AND FARTHER AWAY FROM THE WILL OF GOD IN YOUR LIFE, YOU ARE NOW A FALLEN ANGEL, YOU HAVE FALLEN AWAY FROM THE VERY THING THAT IN ALL THE YEARS BEFORE HAD GIVEN YOU STRENGTH, YOUR FAITH.

IN TITUS 1;16 THEY PROFESS TO KNOW GOD BUT THERE ACTIONS ARE DISOBEDIENT AND WHAT DOES DISOBEDIENTENCE BRING, PAIN, LIES, UNFORGIVENESS, OTHER SCRIPTURES YOU MAY WANT TO CHECK OUT ARE 1 JOHN 2;15-17 2 PETER 2-9 ROMANS 12-2 LUKE 21;34

THE FRIEND WE NEED TO SEEK IN TIMES OF TROUBLE IS JESUS AND ONLY JESUS, HE WILL NEVER LEAVE YOU AND IF YOU TRULY BELIVE IN HIM YOU ALSO KNOW THAT WHAT EVER YOU DO, WHERE EVER YOU GO HE IS RIGHT BESIDE YOU, SITTING IN THAT EMPTY CHAIR NEXT TO YOU, WATCHING AND LISTENING TO YOUR EVERY WORD.

WE HAVE TO HOLD TIGHT TO DEUTERONMY 31;6 WE HAVE TO BE STRONG AND BE OF GOOD COURAGE, NOT BE IN FEAR FOR HE GOES WITH YOU, SO WHAT DO WE DO WHEN WE ARE HURT, WHAT DO WE DO WITH THE PAIN? 1ST PETER 3;8-11 WE HAVE TO REMEMBER AND HOLD TIGHT TO GODS WORD, HE HAS EVERY ANSWER FOR ANYTHING YOU MAY GO THROUGH.

OK SO LETS SAY YOU HAVE DONE THIS, YOU HAVE GONE DOWN THE WRONG PATH AND LEFT YOUR FAITH SORT OF BE PUT BACK IN THE BACK OF A DRAWER, ITS TIME TO GET IT BACK

OUT, FIRST READ THIS WITH ME PSALM 86;5-7

GOD IS READY TO FORGIVE, ALL YOU HAVE TO DO IS CALL ON HIM, IN THE DAY OF MY TROUBLE I WILL CALL UPON YOU FOR YOU WILL ANSWER, PSALM 119;67-68 IT SAYS I WENT ASTRAY BUT NOW I KEEP YOUR WORD, AND AT THE END..TEACH ME YOUR STATUTES IN OTHER WORDS TEACH ME YOUR WAYS THAT THEY BECOME LIKE STONE CARVED IN MY HEART.

THAT IN TIMES OF TROUBLE, PAIN, ANGER GODS WORDS WILL COME OUT NOT THE WORLDS WORDS, THAT LOVE AND FORGIVNESS WILL FLOW FROM YOUR HEART AND YOUR MIND AND IN THAT YOU WILL FIND TRUE PEACE.

IF YOU HAVE GONE THROUGH THINGS IN YOUR LIFE THAT HAVE LEFT YOU FEELING EMPTY, ALONE, MISUNDERSTOOD, WITH A BROKEN HEART, UNFORGIVNESS, FULL OF ANGER, PLEASE AND I PRAY THIS WITH MY WHOLE HEART, DON'T LET THE DEVIL HAVE YOU BACK.

BE STRONG, CALL ON YOUR CHRISTIAN FRIENDS, YOUR CHURCH LEADER, BUT FIRST AND MOST OF ALL CALL ON GOD FOR YOUR STRENGTH, TO FILL YOU WITH HIS SPIRIT SO MUCH THAT ALL YOU FEEL IS HIS PRESENCE WITH YOU. THEN YOU WILL NEVER FEEL SO ALONE THAT YOU REACH BACK OUT TO THE WORLD FOR YOUR COMFORT.

I SPEAK TO YOU WITH A HEART THAT KNOWS, I WENT THROUGH WHAT YOU HAVE, AND ALLOWED THE DEVIL TO HAVE ME BACK, AT THAT TIME IN MY LIFE I WAS NO LONGER SERVEING THE GREAT AND LOVING GOD THAT HAD SAVED ME.

I SERVED THE DEVIL FOR A FEW YEARS BEFORE FINDING MY WAY BACK, AND GOD WAS SO VERY FORGIVING, HE NOT ONLY FORGIVE ME HE ALLOWED ME TO HAVE A SPIRIT OF FORGIVNESS IN ME TOO.

IN FORGIVING I WAS ABLE TO HAVE STRENGTH AGAIN, GOD NEVER LEFT ME I HAD LEFT HIM, AND HE WAS STANDING THERE WITH OPEN ARMS TO TAKE ME RIGHT BACK INTO HIS ARMS, NOTHING YOU DO IS SO BAD YOU WONT BE TAKEN BACK INTO HIS MERCY, HIS GRACE, ALL YOU HAVE TO DO IS ASK.

MY PRAYERS AND HEART GO OUT TO ALL OF YOU THAT

READ THIS, YOUNG AND OLD ALIKE HAVE FALLEN AT ONE TIME OR ANOTHER, STRONG CHRISTIAN, NEW CHRISTIAN, LEADER AND SERVER, BUT IT ISNT EVER TO LATE TO COME BACK. ALL MY LOVE TO YOU AND MAY GOD LEAD YOU TO READ THIS AND COME BACK TO HIM, HE THERE WAITING.

To see other things I have been doing you can check out my websites at

MY WEBSITES
http://www.forministry.com/USMONONDENBMNB/

http://susiesunshine.ning.com/

BOOKS YOU CAN ORDER

http://www.amazon.com/dp/1451286252/ref=tsm_1_fb_lk
Your Transformation into A Butterfly

http://www.amazon.com/Beginnings-Ministry-Min-Susan-Moll/dp/1449071279/ref=sr_1_10?s=books&ie=UTF8&qid=1326727736&sr=1-10

New Beginnings Ministry

Email address dragonfly5918@sbcglobal.net

where you can write for information on topics or books

LuLu pubishing

"Finding Your Healing"

and also "New Beginning's Ministry" revised and redone

the one is my first article I wrote for the Perryville, Mo news paper in 1997 for the ministers corner, the other is clipping for book signing for both of the books. The one for painting is the sunset one in paintings.

at this age I painted the dog

working at tour home in Ste Genevieve I make all my own clothes

worked at nursing homes and in home care for 15 years

day I got author's copy in mail   the pendent I found,

first book signing in 2010 / article I wrote for 3 lumps gone through prayer.

My sweet husband, Tommy Moll, love him with all my heart

PAINTINTING'S FROM 2000 TO 2003

" Sunset over the lake."
Won best of show at fair in Mt Ida Arkansas

HEAVEN AWAITS   2006 to now, still adding

my vision of heaven with all my family and every pet warm springs & all at peace

CHRISTMAS MAGIC   **2001**

DAY FISHING REMEMBERED   2002

HIDDEN LADY, can you find her   1997

SOLITUDE   2001

SPIRIT WITHIN   2002

VISION WITH THE WOLF   2000

POEMS FROM THE HEART THATS HEALING

THE TIME HAS COME

..The time has come to let go of the past, and believe in your heart, you are free at last.
.you trust your heart not to let you down, to guide you within, and keep your feet on the ground,..you have memories of your life, not so good in your mind,
when the one you love hurts you and was bitter, not kind.
.You're afraid to trust, afraid to try, you pray for answers and then start to cry.
.to trust your heart and keep your honor.
.is like going into battle, front line with no armor.
.but you see the light at the end of the tunnel,
your head starts to spin as if falling down a funnel.
..you find at the end, your reborn and anew,
..the old life is gone, ,the cloudy skies have turned blue.
life is full of changes, some good and some bad.
.not all things are painful, your heart can be glad.
.the choices you make now ,will change your life forever,
one day at a time, only getting better,.

I JUST WROTE A LETTER

I just wrote a letter with words straight from the heart, the only question is, where do I start.

The words I write, the feelings I feel, are they love or just caring? They feel so real.

I have to be careful not to scare you away, I never wish to do that, I want you to stay.

So I choose my words carefully, with feeling and thought, with my heart full of happiness and peace you have bought.

I care or I love, the feeling so strong, when held in your arms, nothing seems wrong.

I feel such emotion, I feel I could shout. But carefully and slowly, I write them all out.

2-23-08 NEW POEM BY SUSIE MOLL

" A REASON TO TRY

" I tried to be happy for others to see,when fear and loneliness were inside of me. I tried to help others, and tried to be strong, when I was needing held and protected, is that wrong? My heart was hurting, I felt so alone. I didn't feel comfort where I used to call home. I needed to be held, as a child and let cry, the pain sometimes so deep I felt I could die. Then I looked at my children, the love in their eyes, they gave me tomorrow,and a reason to try. –

By Susie.6-09 . TEAR'S OF THE PAST

As I sit here and think, over all of my life, the tears and the fears,the pain in your heart,that cuts like a knife. You try to find blame ,in all those around,you cry out in the darkness,but no one hears a sound. you don't see the hand that reaches out of the blue, with arms outstretched and reaching around you, My God has been there in all of my pain,the times in my life,I was close to insane. He is my comfort,my strength,in all that I do, He is the only one,that has love so true . He is the love of my life,still not perfect by far, but He loves me anyway, and there's never a scar. His love is deep,His love is wide,and in all of my life,He has been by my side. (for the love of my Jesus) by Susie

(Reflections).. 12-7-07 by Susie..

(Reflections).. As I pray and I think, of all the pain of my life, and now to be free, and not have the strife. to be filled with love and joy down deep in my soul, for the first time in my life,to really feel whole. the pain was for lessons ,that I had to learn, sometimes even God has to be stern. now to see the happiness, only He can give, when you decide to follow Jesus,you learn how to live. to wake in the morning,and know God is inside, there is nothing in your life that you have to try and hide. you feel pure in thought,words and deed,you goal is now to plant those seeds. the seeds of hope,faith and trust,to find your reasons,before turning back to dust. reasons why your here in this time and this space,its to prepare us to meet the lord,face to face... --

2-23-08 POEM BY SUSIE "YOUR NOT HERE,BUT YOU ARE

" Your not here but you are,your in my heart, as in the sky is the north star. Your not here in person,near to the touch. but your inside my heart, I love you so much. Jesus is so wonderful, so gentle and kind, so loving and tender,he never leaves my mind. I talk about him to others, and happiness fills my soul. The heart that was shattered to pieces, now has become whole. The Lord Jesus has blessed me, more than for told. I feel this inside,and will till I am old... --thank you Jesus

' MY LIFE IS A PUZZLE"

My life is a puzzle, but some pieces gone,
the pieces were hope, love and song.
My hope for happiness I found in your eyes,
you fill up my heart, as the stars fill the skies.
Love was missing, sadness filled my soul,
but your touch makes me warm, you make me feel whole.
The song in my heart,sings only your name
you have finished the puzzle, my life will

never be the same...quotation by me..
Life is a puzzle..your friends are the pieces.
When love is found,..the puzzle becomes a work of art.
by Susie 1996

----(As the children cry)---

--THE WORLD REVOLVES AS THE DAYS GO BY,THE WORLD IS SILENT AS THE CHILDREN CRY, WE FEED OTHER COUNTRYS AND WATCH OURS DIE, THE WORLD IS SILENT AS THE CHILDREN CRY.
WE SELL OUR OIL AND SELL OUR GRAIN,WE PRAY FOR PEACE,AND GET ASID RAIN.
WE DESTROY OUR LAND,AND KILL OUR TREES,THE WORLD IS AT LOSE AND FULL OF DISEASE,THE WORLD REVOLVES AND OUR DAYS GO BY ,LISTEN TO YOUR HEARTS,AS THE CHILDREN CRY.
REACH OUT YOUR HAND AS THEY SHED THEIR TEARS, EASE THERE PAIN,AS THEY KNOW SOMEONE IS NEAR..............LET THIS YEAR BE A BLESSING FOR YOU AS WELL AS OTHERS,...REACH OUT

.2-23-08 NEW POEM,. BY Susie.

BEING TRANSFORMED,

Why has this been so very important in my own Ministry and why has God laid it in my heart so strong. The why's are the reason for this study,

Transform;

Php 3:21 who will transform our lowly body that it may be conformed to His glorious body, according to the working by which He is able even to subdue all things to Himself.

Transformed;

Rom 12:2 And do not be conformed to this world, but be transformed by the renewing of your mind, that you may prove what *is* that good and acceptable and perfect will of God.

2Co 3:18 But we all, with unveiled face, beholding as in a mirror the glory of the Lord, are being transformed into the same image from glory to glory, just as by the Spirit of the Lord.

Transforms;

2Co 11:14 And no wonder! For Satan himself transforms himself into an angel of light.

WEBSTERS DICTIONARY;

TRANSFORM', v.t. [L. trans and format.]

1. To change the form of; to change the shape or appearance; to metamorphose; as a caterpillar transformed into a butterfly.
2. To change one substance into another; to transmute. The alchemists sought to transform lead into gold.
3. In theology, to change the natural disposition and temper of man from a state of enmity to God and his law, into the image of God, or into a disposition and temper conformed to the will of God.
Be ye transformed by the renewing of your mind. Rom 12.
4. To change the elements, bread and wine, into the flesh and blood of Christ.
5. Among the mystics, to change the contemplative soul into a divine substance, by which it is lost or swallowed up in the divine nature.
6. In algebra, to change an equation into another of a different form, but of equal value.

TRANSFORM', v.i. To be changed in form; to be metamorphosed.

His hair transforms to down.
Transformation
TRANSFORMA'TION, n. The act or operation of changing the form or external appearance.
1. **Metamorphosis; change of form in insects; as from a caterpillar to a butterfly.**
2. Transmutation; the change of one metal into another, as of copper or tin into gold.
3. The change of the soul into a divine substance, as among the mystics.
4. Transubstantiation. ..**Transubstantiation**
TRANSUBSTANTIA'TION, n. Change of substance. In the Romansh theology, the supposed conversion of the bread and wine in the Eucharist, into the body and blood of Christ.
5. In theology, a change of heart in man, by which his disposition and temper are conformed to the divine image; a change from enmity to holiness and love.
6. In algebra, the change of an equation into one of a different form, but of equal value.
Transformed
TRANSFORM'ED, pp. Changed in form or external appearance; metamorphosed; transmuted; renewed.
Transfiguration
TRANSFIGURA'TION, n.
1. A change of form; particularly, the supernatural change in the personal appearance of our Savior on the mount.
See Mat 17.
2. A feast held by the Romansh church on the 6th of August, in commemoration of the miraculous change above mentioned.
Transfigure
TRANSFIG'URE, v.t. [L. trans and figural.] To transform; to change the outward form or appearance.
--And was transfigured before them. Mat 17.
Transfigured
TRANSFIG'URED, pp. Changed in form.

  So many things have been going through my mind the past few months,

I have been working on getting my book's for my book signing and was checking them out for flaws.

What I saw in all of them were the words being transformed, it was a word I saw on some of the covers, the passages, descriptions of things that happened with me, God what are you really trying to tell me?

Had I got His message or was He still trying so hard to show me something that I was missing, I need to search deep to find out,

Transformed;

Rom 12:2 And do not be conformed to this world, but be transformed by the renewing of your mind, that you may prove what *is* that good and acceptable and perfect will of God.

Okay I knew this one by heart, I knew you had to change your way of thinking for the body to line up and follow, I go about this by reading the bible, there you find the correct way, Jesus way.

By digging deep in the word you find stories about when Jesus was on the earth and going through so many of the very things we do daily, what was His spirit, what were His actions and words.

When you go through something close to this in your own life you will remember what you read, your way of thinking will slowly become like his, study to show yourself approved.

In my study I find this; I. Concerning our duty to God, We see what is godliness.

1. It is to surrender ourselves to God, and so to lay a good foundation. We must first give our own selves unto the Lord, 2Co 8:5. This is here pressed as the spring of all duty and obedience, Rom 12:1, Rom 12:2. Man consists of body and soul, Gen 2:7; Ecc 12:7.
2. (1.) The body must be presented to him, Rom 12:1. *The body is for the Lord, and the Lord for the body,* 1Co 6:13, 1Co 6:14. The exhortation is here introduced very pathetically: *I beseech you, brethren.* Though he was a great apostle, yet he calls the meanest Christians *brethren,* a term of affection and concern. He uses entreaty; this is the gospel way: *As though God did beseech you by us,* 2Co 5:20. Though he might with authority command, yet for love's sake he rather beseeches, Phm 1:8, Phm 1:9. The *poor user entreaty,* Pro 18:23. This is to insinuate the exhortation, that it might come with the more pleasing power. Many are

sooner wrought upon if they be accosted kindly, are more easily led than driven. Now observe,[1.] The duty pressed - to present our *bodies a living sacrifice,* alluding to the sacrifices under the law, which were presented or set before God at the altar, ready to be offered to him. *Your bodies* - your whole selves; so expressed because under the law the bodies of beasts were offered in sacrifice,Our bodies and spirits are intended. The offering was sacrificed by the priest, but presented by the offer-er, who transferred to God all his right, title, and interest in it, by laying his hand on the head of it. Sacrifice is here taken for whatsoever is by God's own appointment dedicated to himself; 1Pe 2:5. We are temple, priest, and sacrifice, as Christ was in his peculiar sacrificing. There were sacrifices of atonement and sacrifices of acknowledgment. Christ, who was once offered to bear the sins of many, is the only sacrifice of atonement; but our persons and performances, tendered to God through Christ our priest, are as sacrifices of acknowledgment to the honor of God. It must be a free-will offering.

God loves you so very much, but He is also a Gentleman, He will not force you to love Him or serve Him. You have a free will and you will have to come willingly to Him,

You come to Him with open arms, unarmed into the loving arms of Jesus, you lay everything down and say I am yours, this old life I want to be gone, forgive me, my past and the sins in my life, mold me into your vessel, take this body and make it yours, teach me your ways.

(Rom 12:2): "*Be you transformed by the renewing of your mind;* see to it that there be a saving change wrought in you, and that it be carried on." Conversion and sanctification are the renewing of the mind, a change not of the substance, but of the qualities of the soul. It is the same with making a new heart and a new spirit - new dispositions and inclinations, new sympathies and antipathies; the understanding enlightened, the conscience softened, the thoughts rectified; the will bowed to the will of God, and the affections made spiritual and heavenly: so that the man is not what he was - old things are passed away, all things are become new; he acts from new principles, by new rules, with new designs. The mind is the acting ruling part of us; so that the renewing of the mind is the renewing of the whole man, for out of it are the *issues of life,*

    Why has God always seemed to use butterflies to talk to me, I looked up how they transform, **TRANSFORMA'TION**, *n. The act or operation of changing the form or external appearance.*

1. **Metamorphosis; change of form in insects; as from a caterpillar to a butterfly.**

    So *I see now its the butterfly being changed He wanted me to see, we are as the worm(in our sinful life) as we come to Jesus we start our cocoon with the word being our weave, we stay in the word(cocooning) feeding off it to grow, to be transformed, then as we grow we are now ready to become the beautiful creatures were suppose to be.*

    As a butterfly what do they do? They go from one place to another spreading the seeds (pollen) to make things grow, in the same way as we have grown and learned lessons to grow, we are to spread our seeds of knowledge to those around us.

    God has used these beautiful creatures to show me when His blessing would be on a move, has used the transformation idea in so many of my lessons and devotions, and when my mom gave me these two pins a lady gave her that topped it off.

    I had gone to visit mom at her apartment and after we had really long talk she said I want you to have something, the lady I got these from was in the labor room with me when I was getting ready to deliver you.

    She went in her room and came out with these two little gold pins, little butterflies, from the very moment I came into the world God had a plan for my life, I would take many paths to find my purpose.

    I know so many times it was hard for God to watch His child go through these times, times I had to do things my way, times I allowed others to pull me in ways that I knew were not of God.

    All I know at this point in my life is God has me and I am hanging on for dear life from here on out, I will never allow anyone or anything to pull me away again.

The transformation isn't complete yet, I am being changed everyday, every second of the day, transformation is really never finished, we are going to be changing as we grow.

With every seed that is sown into our lives it brings about change, every time I go to church and my pastor feeds me a new seed of wisdom I grow, I learn a lesson and am transformed once again.

The last thing in our journey is **TRANSFIG'URE**, To transform; to change the outward form or appearance.
--And was transfigured before them. Mat 17.

Mat 17:1 Now after six days Jesus took Peter, James, and John his brother, led them up on a high mountain by themselves;

Mat 17:2 and He was **transfigured** before them. His face shone like the sun, and His clothes became as white as the light.

Mat 17:3 And behold, Moses and Elijah appeared to them, talking with Him.

Mat 17:4 Then Peter answered and said to Jesus, "Lord, it is good for us to be here; if You wish, let us make here three tabernacles: one for You, one for Moses, and one for Elijah."

Mat 17:5 While he was still speaking, behold, a bright cloud overshadowed them; and suddenly a voice came out of the cloud, saying, "This is My beloved Son, in whom I am well pleased. Hear Him!"

Mat 17:6 And when the disciples heard *it,* they fell on their faces and were greatly afraid.

Mat 17:7 But Jesus came and touched them and said, "Arise, and do not be afraid."

Mat 17:8 When they had lifted up their eyes, they saw no one but Jesus only.

Mat 17:9 Now as they came down from the mountain, Jesus commanded them, saying, "Tell the vision to no one until the Son of Man is risen from the dead."

Mat 17:10 And His disciples asked Him, saying, "Why then do the scribes say that Elijah must come first?"

Mat 17:11 Jesus answered and said to them, "Indeed, Elijah is coming

first and will restore all things.
Mat 17:12 But I say to you that Elijah has come already, and they did not know him but did to him whatever they wished. Likewise the Son of Man is also about to suffer at their hands."
Mat 17:13 Then the disciples understood that He spoke to them of John the Baptist.
Mat 17:14 And when they had come to the multitude, a man came to Him, kneeling down to Him and saying,
Mat 17:15 "Lord, have mercy on my son, for he is an epileptic and suffers severely; for he often falls into the fire and often into the water.
Mat 17:16 So I brought him to Your disciples, but they could not cure him."
Mat 17:17 Then Jesus answered and said, "O faithless and perverse generation, how long shall I be with you? How long shall I bear with you? Bring him here to Me."
Mat 17:18 And Jesus rebuked the demon, and it came out of him; and the child was cured from that very hour.
Mat 17:19 Then the disciples came to Jesus privately and said, "Why could we not cast it out?"
Mat 17:20 So Jesus said to them, "Because of your unbelief; for assuredly, I say to you, if you have faith as a mustard seed, you will say to this mountain, 'Move from here to there,' and it will move; and nothing will be impossible for you.
Mat 17:21 However, this kind does not go out except by prayer and fasting."

At the time of our death we too will be transfigured, our bodies that are broken, hurting, with things seen and unseen that may not be the way they were designed. Will transform into being made perfect, as we go to heaven we will have bodies that will be whole in every way.

Up to this point the transformation has been on the inside, not on the outside, oh you may have cleaned up if your life was really bad before, you may now view your body as a true temple and care for it better and maybe be healthier, habits have been taken away that were harming you.

But upon death you will have a body that goes along with the spirit you now have, all things will come together and be the creation you were made to be. Oh that day of rapture when the new Heaven will come, our transformation complete we will live with Jesus forever and ever.

The information I have used is the NKJV with Henry's commentary

Pins from my Momma

learning to relax with husband and enjoy just being alive and all God has made

day of fishing, 6-9-12   our 5th anniversary

Our 5th anniversary, so special for both of us, they have been good and bad years for us in so many ways, but everything has been side by side, that is the way it will stay, as we go through our years to come I know there will be trials that will seem at times to be to much.

But God has promised never to give us more than we can handle, knowing that all we go through has first past through His hands, He has our answers, our healing s. If we believe, if we trust. If we hang on to one more day and never give up.

We have some health issues coming up that will be a real test for us, but I will never let go of Gods hand or Toms, I have found the man God created just for me and I for him, and it will be till death do us part.

I don't know what you see, but what Tom and I saw was God forming a heart right over the area where we sat, as the wind blew the other half formed and went away.
Another God moment in my chapters of life

NOTES

NOTES

© 2012 by Minister Susan K Moll.

All rights reserved. No part of this book may be reproduced, stored in a retrieval system or transmitted in any form or by any means without the prior written permission of the writer except by a reviewer who may quote brief passages in a review to be printed in a news paper, magazine or journal.

First printing 2012

ISBN 978-1-105-87986-9

NOTES